PRAYER

LORD, TEACH US TO PRAY,

A Journey Into The Heart of Intimacy With God

DR. LEE A. SIMPSON

Contents

To every reader

who dares to seek Him deeply—

may these words stir your spirit,

strengthen your faith,

and draw you into continual communion

with the God who still speaks.

May each page become a doorway into His presence,

a reminder that prayer is not merely spoken—

it is lived.

This book is for every heart

that has ever whispered, with longing and love,

"Lord, teach me to pray."

And for every soul still learning

that the greatest prayers

are not recited from memory,

but breathed from intimacy.

PREFACE

There are moments when heaven comes so close that something inside you knows it. The air shifts. The heart settles. And without effort, you become aware of a Presence you could never deserve, yet you are invited to receive. I have lived long enough to know that those moments are not random. They are God's way of whispering, "Come closer... I'm here."

This book was born in the quiet places—before the sun was up, when the house was still and the world had not yet started pulling on my attention. It came in those moments when I slipped into the presence of God not to preach, not to perform, but simply to be a son talking to his Father.

Over the years, I have stood in pulpits, sat in counseling sessions, prayed at hospital bedsides, and walked with people through some of the hardest moments of their lives. I have seen God answer prayers in ways that took my breath away. I have also walked through seasons where heaven seemed silent and I had more questions than answers. Yet through it all, one truth has held me: God listens when His children pray.

What you hold in your hands did not come from a desire to add another title to a shelf. It came from a burden I could not shake. I began to notice a pattern in the lives of many believers—faithful people who loved God, attended church, knew Scripture, and yet quietly struggled in the area of prayer. Some felt intimidated, unsure if they were "doing it right." Others were discouraged, worn out from praying with little visible change. Still others were simply busy and distracted, intending to pray more "one day," but rarely finding the time.

At the same time, I could not ignore how fiercely the enemy fights prayer. It is not by accident that the mind wanders most when you try to pray, that fatigue sets in when you decide to seek God more, or that resistance rises when you determine to build a real prayer life. If prayer were ordinary, the enemy would leave it alone. The battle that surrounds prayer is proof of its power.

As I revisited familiar stories in Scripture—Daniel in the lions' den, his three friends in the fiery furnace, the delayed answer to Daniel's prayer, and Jesus' own teachings on prayer—I saw something with fresh clarity: prayer is not a side topic in the Christian life. It is the lifeline. It is how you walk with God, how you receive His help, and how you partner with His purposes in the earth.

That realization would not leave me. I found myself praying, "Lord, Your people know they should pray, but many don't understand what prayer truly is. Help me write in a way that lifts the weight, removes the fear, and opens the door for them to come closer."

This book is my answer to that prayer.

I wrote these pages with a pastor's heart and a fellow traveler's honesty. I do not write as someone who has mastered prayer, but as someone who has been mastered by the awareness that I cannot live without it. I have learned, sometimes the hard way, that activity without prayer is emptiness dressed in motion. I have also tasted the deep rest and unshakable strength that come when prayer is no longer an afterthought but a way of life.

As you read, my desire is not to impress you with insights, but to walk beside you and invite you deeper. I want you to see that prayer is not reserved for "special" Christians. It is not about having perfect words or flawless focus. Prayer is about relationship—with a Father who loves you, a Savior who intercedes for you, and the Holy Spirit who helps you when you don't even know what to say.

These pages will speak about the purpose of prayer—why God designed it and why you were never meant to live without it. They will unfold the privilege of prayer—the astonishing reality that you are welcomed, not tolerated, in the presence of Almighty God. And they will explore the power of prayer—how your time with God changes situations, but more importantly, changes you.

You will see that when Daniel refused to stop praying, heaven did not ignore his faithfulness—God met him in the lions' den. When his three friends refused to bow, God met them in the fire. And when Daniel set his heart to seek understanding, heaven heard him from the very first day, even though the answer was delayed by unseen opposition. These are not just ancient stories; they are windows into how God still moves in response to prayer.

My prayer for you as you hold this book is simple: that something inside you will begin to hunger for more. Not more information about prayer, but more encounters with God in prayer. That you will discover—or rediscover—that prayer is not a performance to endure, but a place to belong. That you will come to see prayer not as a duty that drains you, but as a lifeline that sustains you.

If by the time you finish this book, your heart quietly whispers, "Lord, teach me to pray," then the purpose for which I wrote it will be fulfilled. Because that simple cry—the same cry the disciples brought to Jesus—opens the door to a journey that will transform your walk with God.

From my heart to yours, I invite you to take that journey. Let's go together into the school of the Spirit, where the Lord Himself will answer the cry of every willing heart:

"Lord, teach us to pray."

INTRODUCTION

THE RETURN TO PRESENCE

Prayer has never been a small thing.

It is not a comfort habit for the weak, nor a religious duty for the "super-spiritual." Prayer is the place where heaven and earth meet, where God's heart and your heart come into agreement. It is conversation, yes—but it is also communion, partnership, and warfare all at once.

I have lived long enough, and prayed through enough seasons, to know this much: nothing in the Christian life works the way it should without a living, growing life of prayer. Salvation introduces you to God. Prayer keeps you walking with Him.

And because prayer is this important, it is also this contested.

If prayer were ordinary—just "talking into the air"—the enemy would ignore it. Instead, he fights it. He distracts you when you try to pray. He weighs you down when you decide to seek God more deeply. He whispers that it "doesn't work" when answers seem delayed. All of this is evidence of how powerful prayer truly is.

This book was born out of that reality. It is my way of walking beside you and saying, "You are not crazy. You really are in a battle over your prayer life. But you are not powerless, and you are not alone."

THE PURPOSE OF PRAYER

You were created for a relationship with God.

Not religion. Not routine. Relationship.

From the garden of Eden to the New Testament church, God's desire has always been the same: to dwell with His people, to walk with them, to talk with them. Prayer is the God-given way you step into that fellowship.

Prayer is how you:

Share your heart with your Father.

Listen for His voice, guidance, and correction.

Align your will with His will.

Partner with Him in what He is doing in the earth.

When Daniel opened his windows toward Jerusalem and prayed three times a day, he was not checking off a religious box. He was living from the purpose for which he was created—to seek God, to honor Him, and to stay in communion with Him, no matter the cost.

The purpose of prayer is not to impress God, but to walk with Him. It is not to convince Him to care, but to agree with what He already desires to do in you and through you.

THE PRIVILEGE OF PRAYER

The privilege of prayer is easy to forget when life is busy and pressure is high. Yet Scripture reminds you of something astonishing: you are invited to come boldly before the throne of grace. Not as a stranger. Not as a beggar. As a son or daughter.

Daniel's enemies passed a law to stop him from praying. They understood something many believers overlook: his strength, wisdom, and favor flowed from his relationship with God. If they could cut off his access, they could cripple his life.

They underestimated the God he served.

When Daniel chose prayer over safety, he was thrown into the lions' den. From the outside, it looked like the end. From heaven's view, it was a stage. God sent an angel to shut the mouths of the lions. The very place designed to destroy him became a testimony to the God who hears and responds.

The same is true of Daniel's three friends. They refused to bow to Nebuchadnezzar's golden statue. They chose loyalty to God over survival in a system that wanted their worship. They ended up in a fiery furnace—but they did not burn. Instead, the Fourth Man, the Son of God, showed up in the flames.

What does that have to do with you?

Everything.

You live in a world that gladly offers substitutes for prayer: distraction, entertainment, busyness, even religious activity without relationship. Yet in every season, your Father is whispering, "Come to Me. Talk to Me. Walk with Me."

Prayer is not a burden He throws at you. It is a privilege He opens to you. You are welcomed into the same Presence that shut the lions' mouths and walked in the fire.

THE POWER OF PRAYER

Prayer does not just change things; prayer changes you.

When Daniel fasted and prayed for understanding, the answer from heaven was sent on the very first day. Yet for twenty-one days, a demonic prince resisted the angel who carried that answer. What started as prayer in Daniel's room became a battle in the invisible realm.

That story reveals something important: prayer has weight in the spirit. Your words before God matter. Your persistence matters. Your "yes" to prayer stirs movement in realms you cannot see.

This is why Jesus said in Luke 18:1 that you "ought always to pray and not lose heart." Prayer is not a one-time event; it is a life posture. It is choosing to keep talking to God when you feel nothing, when you see nothing, and when the battle seems long.

Prayer carries power because:

It brings heaven's will into earthly situations.

It pushes back darkness and confusion.

It opens your life to the Holy Spirit's strength, comfort, and wisdom.

It transforms your heart, your desires, and your perspective.

A prayerless believer is an easy target.

A praying believer is not.

When you pray, you become rooted. The storms still come, but you do not topple as easily. Fear still tries to speak, but faith speaks louder. The enemy still attacks, but you are no longer standing in your own strength; you are standing in God's.

WHY THIS BOOK

This book is an invitation to rediscover prayer—not as a duty to endure, but as a relationship to enjoy, a privilege to cherish, and a power to walk in daily.

As you read, you will:

See why the enemy works so hard to fight your prayer life.

Learn the purpose of prayer as partnership with God, not performance for Him.

Discover the privilege of coming before God as Father, not as a distant Judge.

Experience the power of persevering prayer, even when you feel like giving up.

My desire is simple: that by the time you finish this book, your heart will whisper what the disciples once said to Jesus, not as a phrase, but as a cry:

"Lord, teach us to pray."

And as you walk through these pages, I believe He will.

A MORNING THAT RESET MY HEART

Before these pages were ever outlined, there was a morning that marked me.

The previous night had stretched late, and when the first light crept into the sky, I was caught somewhere between fatigue and quiet pondering. A thin veil of moisture rested in the air outside my office window, and the early gray of daybreak carried a calm that felt almost like a sanctuary.

There were no dramatic signs. No flashes of lightning. Just a gentle movement of air across the trees, as if creation itself had paused. I sat there with my Bible open and a cup of coffee beside me growing cooler by the minute, and for the first time in a while, I realized I had run out of words.

The previous weeks had been full—ministry, preaching, counseling, leading. I kept pouring out, again and again. I still believed every word I preached, but deep inside, the sharp edge of wonder had begun to dull. My faith was active, yet the nearness that only comes from lingering in His presence had quietly grown thin.

So that morning, I lowered my head—not to speak, but to be still. In that quiet, He drew near. There was no shaking of the room, no outward sign, yet I became deeply aware of His nearness: gentle, patient, waiting. The same Presence I had proclaimed to others was now reaching for me—not to assign another task, but to draw me back into simple fellowship.

It did not come as a rebuke. It came as a tender pull. A phrase rose within my heart like a soft embrace:

"I've missed you."

Tears surfaced before any sentences formed. I saw how faithfully I had served while allowing my own heart to drift. I had offered God my energy, but not my unhurried attention. My calendar belonged to Him, but my quiet spaces were crowded. Still, He came close.

That day, my prayer did not sound polished. It sounded empty and honest. I was not trying to impress God; I was admitting how much I needed Him. In that yielding, He met me—not as a far-off ruler, but as a Father whose arms had always been open.

His nearness settled in that room the way light gently breaks through clouds after a storm. A deep calm washed over me. Joy began to rise again. Slowly, I became aware that a burden I hadn't even named was lifting. Deep inside, my heart answered without speech: "I missed You too, Abba."

And in that holy quiet, there was a knowing in my spirit—as clear as if spoken aloud:

"Then stay."

That simple inner nudge became a turning point. It was a call to return—not to constant doing, but to dwelling. Not to performance, but to presence.

THE HEART OF THIS JOURNEY

What happened that morning became the well from which this book flows. The chapters you are about to read grew out of that renewed nearness—the fresh awareness of walking closely with the Holy Spirit again.

As you step into this journey, I want to talk to you as a pastor and a fellow traveler.

The opening chapter on adoration is intentionally longer than the others because it lays the groundwork for everything that follows. Adoration is not a side topic; it is the doorway into the kind of prayer life your heart has been craving.

Take your time with that chapter. Move through it slowly. Let the sentences invite you into a quieter place inside. If it feels like too much to absorb at once, receive it in smaller portions. Pause whenever you sense the Holy Spirit drawing your attention to a phrase or stirring something within you.

Set aside a space where you can be alone for a while. Turn away from the noise for a moment. Before you begin reading in earnest, breathe a simple request:

"Lord, speak to my heart."

If you walk through this book with your inner life engaged—and not just your intellect—what you learn will not stay on the page. Your conversations with God will shift. Your confidence in Him will grow. A deeper hunger for His nearness will begin to awaken.

More than anything, my prayer is that you will discover how to experience the kind of closeness with God your soul has quietly desired for years—even if you could not always name that desire.

These chapters are not built around abstract concepts. They are shaped around real encounters. You are not just observing someone else's story; you are being invited into your own.

STEPPING INTO THE QUIET

What you are holding is not only instruction. It is a doorway.

It is a call back to the uncluttered place. To the calm where God's voice becomes easier to hear. To the inner room where your words eventually fall silent and His presence fills the gap.

Prayer is not a technique to perfect. It is a connection to guard. It is not a cold formula; it is warm fellowship. It is not primarily taught in lecture halls; it is learned in the secret place where you and God meet again and again.

When the disciples watched Jesus pray, they noticed something deeper than His sermons and miracles. They saw how He consistently stepped away from the crowds to spend time alone with the Father, and it became clear that this relationship was the source of His power. They did not ask Him to teach them how to preach or how to perform miracles. What they truly wanted was to share the level of closeness and intimacy with the Father that Jesus had.

In the same way, the Holy Spirit is quietly drawing you. Not with loud demands, but with a steady pull. He has been waiting—not for flawless performance, but for willing nearness.

So, before you move into the first chapter, let yourself pause. Take a slow breath. Allow the grace of God to rest on you like early light after a long night. Lay down yesterday's striving and today's pressure. Right here, between the life you've known and the work God is about to do in you, there is a holy pause.

This is the threshold of change.

This is where closeness with God is renewed.

And this is where our path opens—

with adoration.

CHAPTER 1

ADORATION: THE BREATH OF PRAYER

The room was quiet. Creation seemed to hum softly in the background—subtle, steady, alive. God's presence settled in that silence like a sacred whisper meant for the heart alone, a nearness that could be sensed long before words ever formed. I didn't come with a list. I didn't search for the right phrases. I just sat there in the stillness, heart overflowing, eyes filling with tears that needed no explanation.

Then, in that sacred quiet, the Holy Spirit whispered to my heart, "This is adoration—the purest form of prayer, the foundation upon which every other kind should stand."

It wasn't about asking or declaring. It was about beholding. About slowing down until the noise inside quieted enough for wonder to rise. In that moment, words faded, and worship began. My heart stopped striving and simply sighed, "Lord, You're beautiful."

Over the years, I've learned that adoration is the most powerful, yet often the most neglected, dimension of prayer. We rush to petition, to ask, to intercede—but transformation begins in awe. Before we repent, before we ask, before we stand in the gap, there must first be wonder.

True prayer doesn't begin with words—it begins with worship. It is not found in the length of our prayers, but in the posture of our hearts. When adoration precedes petition, mercy answers swiftly.

THE HUMBLE PRAYER THAT TOUCHED HEAVEN

Jesus told of two men who went up to the temple to pray—one a Pharisee and the other a tax collector. The tax collector stood at a distance, unable even to lift his eyes toward heaven. With his hand beating against his chest, he quietly pleaded, "God, be merciful to me, a sinner" (Luke 18:13, NKJV).

That moment was more than repentance—it was adoration.

Before he formed a sentence, he stood in reverence. Before he confessed, he worshiped. His silence was an offering. His humility was incense rising to heaven.

He felt the weight of God's presence and recognized his own unworthiness. He didn't come to impress heaven with eloquence. He came broken—believing that mercy still flows from the covenant the God of Israel made with His people.

Deep within, he must have remembered the words spoken through the prophet:

"But if a wicked man turns from all his sins which he has committed, keeps all My statutes, and does what is lawful and right, he shall surely live; he shall not die. None of the transgressions which he has committed shall be remembered against him" (Ezekiel 18:21–22, NKJV).

That truth became life to him. In that moment, the man didn't only confess—he connected.

If believers today would approach God with that same reverence—not through the letter of the Law, but through the grace of relationship made possible by the blood of Jesus—we would experience the same nearness of mercy. The cross changed everything. We no longer approach trembling before a Judge; we come boldly before a Father who delights in mercy.

The sinner's whispered cry still echoes as a lesson for us all. Heart-prayer, adoration, doesn't begin with many words—it begins with worship. Heaven responds not to perfection, but to posture. When adoration precedes petition, mercy moves quickly.

Jesus said the sinner left that place justified. God placed him in right standing with Himself, as if he had never sinned. Heaven responded not to the man's religion but to his humility. His posture invited grace. Meanwhile, the Pharisee, polished in his prayers and praised by his peers, left unchanged. His words were lofty, but his heart was far away.

The tax collector's prayer touched heaven because it came from the depths of his heart. The Pharisee, however, stood there boasting about his own goodness, and his prayer never rose above his pride. God is not moved by performance—He desires your heart.

Adoration isn't just how prayer begins—it is the posture that sustains it. It shifts your focus from problems to Presence, from chaos to calm, from anxiety to awe. When you adore, you realign your soul with heaven's rhythm. The atmosphere shifts, because adoration makes room for His glory to dwell where your heart bows low.

Every divine encounter in Scripture began in awe. Isaiah didn't start with, "Here am I; send me." He began with, "I saw the Lord, high and lifted up" (Isaiah 6:1). John didn't receive Revelation through ambition; he fell at Jesus' feet in worship. Even Mary, before she carried the Lord made flesh, magnified the Lord in humble adoration.

Adoration is the soil where revelation grows. It's where you stop telling God about your world and start letting Him reveal His.

WHERE ADORATION BEGINS

Adoration is both simple and profound. It doesn't demand eloquence or education—just an honest heart that knows who God is. Worship often celebrates what God has done; adoration rests in who He is. Worship lifts the hands; adoration bends the heart.

It begins when you turn your gaze from earth to heaven and whisper words of reverence: "Lord, You are holy. You are merciful. You are good." As your mind recalls His nature, gratitude begins to flow like a river—thanking Him for His faithfulness, His patience, His protection, His presence. The more you speak of who He is, the more your heart begins to reflect what heaven already declares.

David captured this hunger when he wrote, "One thing I have desired of the Lord, that will I seek: that I may dwell in the house of the Lord all the days of my life, to behold the beauty of the Lord" (Psalm 27:4, NKJV). To behold is to gaze deeply—to look until what you see transforms you within. That is the essence of adoration. It slows you down until your heart catches up with His presence.

Mary of Bethany understood this. While others rushed to serve and impress, she sat in stillness at Jesus' feet, her soul completely captivated. Her love wasn't loud, but it was pure. Jesus said she had chosen the better part—the one thing that would not be taken from her (Luke 10:38–42).

Adoration pulls you away from the noise of many things and centers you on the one thing. It quiets the anxious heart and awakens the eternal one. The more you adore Him, the smaller your worries seem beside His majesty. The burdens you carry grow light beneath the weight of His glory.

WHEN HEAVEN DRAWS NEAR

Adoration is an invitation for heaven to come close. Scripture says, "But You are holy, enthroned in the praises of Israel" (Psalm 22:3, NKJV). When you adore, you build a throne in your heart for the King to sit upon. Right there—in your room, in your car, in your midnight hour—His presence fills the air, and everything begins to change.

Worry gives way to peace. Fear melts into faith. Weakness is clothed with strength.

There is something sacred about calling Him by His names. When you whisper, "Jehovah Jireh—my Provider," your spirit remembers that He sees and supplies. When you call Him "Jehovah Shalom—my Peace," storms within begin to still. When you declare, "El Shaddai—God Almighty," faith rises, reminding you that no power can rival His strength. Every name unveils a facet of His glory, and every revelation draws your heart closer in adoration.

David discovered this power in the wilderness. He wrote, "O God, You are my God; early will I seek You; my soul thirsts for You, my flesh longs for You in a dry and thirsty land" (Psalm 63:1, NKJV). He wasn't in a palace but a desert—yet even there, worship found him. That's the mystery of adoration—it turns barren places into sanctuaries.

Paul and Silas understood this too. Bound in chains, beaten, and imprisoned, they chose not to wait for freedom before worshiping. At midnight, their voices rose in song, and heaven answered. The earth shook, chains broke, and every door swung open (Acts 16:25–26). Adoration has that kind of power—it shakes the foundations of what has tried to hold you captive.

THE BREATH OF PRAYER

When your heart rises in awe, you join heaven's eternal rhythm. Angels who have never known sin still cry, "Holy, holy, holy, Lord God Almighty, who was and is and is to come" (Revelation 4:8, NKJV). Their praise doesn't come from need but from revelation. They aren't asking for anything—they are beholding everything.

That's what happens when adoration becomes the breath of your prayer life. You stop only seeking what He can do and start gazing at who He is. Prayer becomes less about speaking to God and more about communing with Him.

When Isaiah saw the Lord high and lifted up, he didn't bring a list of requests; awe overtook him. Overwhelmed by glory, he cried, "Woe is me, for I am undone!" (Isaiah 6:5). That trembling moment became his transformation. Adoration reveals both—the holiness of God and the humility of man.

Hannah's story echoes this truth. Her prayer began in anguish but ended in adoration. As she poured out her heart before the Lord, her burden turned into worship. When God answered, her song wasn't about the gift—it was about the Giver: "My heart rejoices in the Lord... there is none holy like the Lord" (1 Samuel 2:1–2). Adoration turns sorrow into song and despair into devotion.

THE POSTURE OF THE HEART

True adoration is not defined by physical position but by inward posture. You can be standing, sitting, or lying prostrate—it is the surrender of the soul that heaven recognizes.

"Oh come, let us worship and bow down; let us kneel before the Lord our Maker" (Psalm 95:6, NKJV). To bow is not only to lower the body—it is to yield the will. It is to say, "You are God, and I am Yours." When you come before Him in adoration, you are not demanding an audience; you are honoring a King who graciously allows you near.

This posture stills the noise of the world. It quiets anxious thoughts and fills the heart with peace. Before I speak a single word, I often whisper, "Father, You are worthy." I let that truth linger in the silence until my heart bows low and His peace rises like dawn.

You may say, "But I don't always feel like worshiping." That's when adoration becomes most powerful. True adoration is not driven by emotion—it's born from revelation. You don't adore because life feels good; you adore because God is good.

The woman with the alabaster box didn't worship because she understood everything—she worshiped because mercy had found her. Every tear that fell was a note in heaven's song. Her devotion wasn't logical; it was love. Jesus said that her act of adoration would be remembered wherever the gospel is preached (Matthew 26:6–13).

Adoration will always cost something—your pride, your plans, your self-consciousness. But whatever you pour out in surrender, God fills with His glory. The fragrance of such worship lingers long after the moment fades.

Maybe your prayers have felt routine lately, your heart weary from repetition. Adoration is the key that reopens the door of delight. When you praise Him simply because He is worthy, your soul begins to breathe again. Passion rekindles. Love revives. His presence becomes tangible.

In adoration, you rediscover the reason you first fell in love with Him.

THE TRANSFORMING POWER OF ADORATION

Adoration does more than move heaven—it transforms you. The more you behold Him, the more you become like Him. In His light, problems lose their weight, fear gives way to faith, and the soul finds rest in the certainty of His goodness.

If you learn to adore before you ask, you will often find peace before the answer arrives. Adoration resets your focus from what is temporary to what is eternal. It quiets the striving and re-centers the heart on the One who holds all things together.

There are those who believe they don't have time to pray, to worship, or to adore. But adoration isn't something you schedule—it's something you live. It isn't confined to pews or prayer closets; it flows from a heart that stays aware of His presence.

You can adore Him in the sanctuary, yes—but you can also adore Him in the kitchen while stirring a pot, folding clothes, or driving through traffic with tears streaming down your face. Adoration is not about a perfect setting; it's about a willing spirit. It's the quiet turning of your heart toward God in the middle of your day, when words fail but love still speaks.

God doesn't respond to volume; He responds to posture. He listens for the sound of humility, the rhythm of gratitude, the whisper of a heart leaning in His direction. When your spirit bows low in awe, even in the simplest moments, heaven bends close to meet you there.

John discovered this on the island of Patmos. Exiled and alone, surrounded by silence and sea, he found himself "in the Spirit on the Lord's Day" (Revelation 1:10). His adoration opened the heavens. Revelation followed. The greatest mysteries of eternity were entrusted to a man who chose worship over worry.

That's the secret—adoration opens what anxiety closes. When you fix your gaze on the King, revelation flows where fear once ruled. In that sacred exchange, your praise ascends, and His presence descends. Heaven recognizes the sound of a heart bowed low.

And when His Spirit begins to move within your worship, you realize something holy: you're not speaking about God anymore—you're speaking with Him. The room becomes a sanctuary, your words become incense, and the moment becomes eternal.

Adoration restores your perspective. In a world that magnifies what's wrong, it reminds you of Who is right. It lifts your eyes from the storm to the Savior, from the news to the Name above every name. It brings your heart back to the truth that God hasn't forgotten you—and He hasn't changed His mind about you.

HOW TO CULTIVATE ADORATION

Adoration grows best in the soil of consistency. It's not an emotion to chase but a discipline to practice. Every time you turn your focus heavenward, you're tilling the ground of your heart to receive His presence.

Here are a few ways to nurture this sacred rhythm:

Begin with gratitude. Start your prayer not with needs, but with thanksgiving. Gratitude clears the heart for reverence and invites His peace to enter.

Let Scripture lead your worship. Read passages like Psalm 103 or Revelation 4 aloud. Allow the Lord to "supply the words" until they become your worship.

Linger in silence. Don't rush to fill every pause. Some of the holiest moments are wordless, where your heart listens more than it speaks.

Create atmosphere. Through music or quiet, make space to remind your soul to meet God.

Acknowledge His nearness. Speak as one who knows He is already there, not as one trying to summon Him. His presence is not earned—it's embraced.

Over time, adoration will become a habit of the heart. It will shape your mornings, steady your emotions, and anchor your faith when the world trembles.

WHEN ADORATION BECOMES COMMUNION

There comes a moment when adoration matures into communion. It is no longer an act—it becomes awareness. You begin to sense His nearness everywhere. His presence is no longer confined to the prayer room; it saturates the ordinary.

You whisper, "Thank You, Lord," in the grocery aisle. You sense His peace while driving through traffic. You feel His hand upon your shoulder when you're weary. This is the hidden gift of adoration—it makes His presence personal and near.

David captured it perfectly: "I have set the Lord always before me; because He is at my right hand I shall not be moved" (Psalm 16:8, NKJV). When your heart remains turned toward Him, everything else aligns.

Adoration is not merely the beginning of prayer—it is the heartbeat of it. Every other form of prayer flows from this fountain. When you adore, your petitions are filled with faith, your intercession with compassion, and your confession with humility. Everything is purified in the fire of worship.

So pause. Don't rush into prayer with your list. Begin with love. Close your eyes. Whisper His name. Tell Him who He is to you. Let your heart rise in awe until the atmosphere around you feels full of His glory.

That's when you realize—adoration is not a prelude to prayer. It is prayer. It is the breath of it.

In that holy stillness, every breath becomes sacred. Every whisper becomes worship. You sense the weight of His presence—not demanding, but drawing. The soul bows low, and heaven bends near. And in that quiet communion, you understand the truth: the highest form of prayer is not petition, but presence.

REFLECTION QUESTIONS

When was the last time you lingered in God's presence simply to adore Him—without an agenda or request?

Which attribute of God is He inviting you to contemplate more deeply in this season?

How can you begin each day by turning your focus from requests to reverence?

What distractions keep you from adoration, and how might the Lord be calling you to overcome them?

PRAYER

Father, teach my heart to adore before I ask. Let my worship rise beyond words until I rest in Your presence. Silence every distraction that competes for my attention and help me remember—You are already near.

May my adoration be the fragrance that fills Your throne room. When I speak, let it be from love; when I am silent, let it be in awe. Turn my gaze fully toward You until everything else fades away.

In Jesus' name, Amen.

COMING NEXT

As adoration deepens, something shifts within—the heart that bows low before God begins to feel His pull toward deeper fellowship. In that quiet stillness, you sense the whisper of the Spirit saying,

"Now that you've turned your heart toward Me... stay."

That is where prayer becomes communion—in **THE SECRET PLACE: WHERE HEAVEN MEETS THE HEART.**

CHAPTER 2

THE SECRET PLACE: WHERE HEAVEN MEETS THE HEART

The morning was quiet, still wrapped in darkness, when I slipped out onto the back patio. Dawn had not yet fully arrived, but the horizon glowed just enough to hint that the sun was on its way. Fresh dew sparkled on the grass like tiny treasures placed there by the Father Himself. The cool air carried a sacred hush—the kind that makes your heart slow down and listen.

Life began moving around me. Squirrels chased each other up and down the oak trees with bursts of playful energy. A rabbit, alert and yet curious, hopped across the yard before slipping beneath the hedge. And from the branches above, birds filled the morning with song—melodies rising and falling like waves of joy rolling across the sky.

I sat there watching them, and a realization settled deep within me. They lived freely. The trees gave them shelter. The earth offered them food. The air carried their song. My yard had become their refuge—a place of safety, provision, and peace. I was their landlord, though they owed me nothing. And my joy came not from what they gave, but simply from watching them live as they were created to live... in rest. All they had to do was abide.

And in that stillness, the Father whispered, "This is how I care for you—only infinitely more."

It was as if creation had preached a silent sermon. Everything around me rested without fear, without striving, without anxiety. Yet I realized how often we, God's children, live with pressure rather than peace—working, fixing, pushing, trying to hold everything together when the Father simply wants us to live in the refuge of His presence. Animals live under His care, but we are invited to live in His heart.

Jesus told us that not one sparrow falls without the Father's attention. Then He said something stunning: "Are you not of more value than they?" (Matthew 6:26). If the Creator cares for every creature He made, how much more does the Father care for His children? His desire isn't just to provide for us but to be with us. To walk with us. To abide with us.

The Father and the Son both use one word to describe the relationship They long to have with us: abide. Not visit. Not check in occasionally. Abide. "Abide in Me, and I in you" (John 15:4). That word is the language of love. It's the rhythm of communion. It's the invitation of a Father who wants His children near.

When birds rest in the trees, they experience provision. When we rest in the Father, we experience presence. One reflects creation. The other reflects covenant.

This is what it means to abide—to live aware of His Spirit within you, guiding, comforting, filling, transforming. The Father doesn't just want to watch over you; He wants to walk with you. Jesus doesn't just sustain you; He invites you into fellowship that satisfies the soul.

The day before that morning, the Holy Spirit had led me to Psalm 91. I prayed, "Father, show me the secret place. Teach me how to enter it... and how to stay." I had always loved that passage for its promises—protection, deliverance, peace—but that day I saw something deeper: every promise in Psalm 91 flows from one condition... dwelling in the secret place of the

Most High.

To dwell is not to visit. It is not to check in occasionally and then withdraw. To dwell is to remain—to make your home in God's presence. Those who dwell are not merely seeking protection; they are cultivating relationship. They live under the shadow of the Almighty through communion, surrender, and trust.

The secret place isn't a location—it's a relationship. It is the place where the heart of a believer intertwines with the heart of God. It is intimacy—not routine, not performance, not obligation, but closeness. No pretense. No pressure. No distance.

This is why Jesus began the Lord's Prayer not with request but with relationship: "Our Father." Before daily bread, before forgiveness, before deliverance, He pointed to identity. He was teaching us that prayer is born from belonging. You cannot truly abide in Someone you fear is distant, unpredictable, or disappointed in you. Intimacy flourishes only where trust lives.

But Jesus shattered the image of a distant deity. He revealed the Father. Not a tyrant. Not a judge waiting for failure. Not a silent monarch hidden behind a throne. A Father who delights in His children. A Father who listens for your voice, who welcomes your tears, who never withdraws His love.

To pray to God as Father is to renounce the lie of abandonment. It is to reject shame and fear. It is to believe you are wanted, chosen, and seen. When you know the Father loves you, abiding becomes natural. You don't force yourself to pray. You find yourself drawn into prayer. Not to perform — but to commune. Not to impress — but to remain.

That morning, as worship began to rise inside me, I felt His presence settle around me like warm sunlight breaking through the coolness of dawn. For weeks, I had been encountering wave after wave of His nearness as He taught me the power of adoration. Every moment of lingering opened a doorway into deeper awareness of Him. Every whisper of praise brought me further into the secret place.

And the more I abided, the more I realized that the greatest reward of prayer is not what you receive — it's who you become. You leave the secret place carrying something unseen yet undeniable — the fragrance of His presence. Peace where there used to be panic. Trust where there used to be tension. Rest where there used to be worry. Public strength is always born in private surrender.

Psalm 91 declares, "He is my refuge and my fortress; My God, in Him I will trust." Trust is the foundation of intimacy. Without trust there can be no peace, and without peace there can be no abiding. To trust the Father is to rest in His heart even when life feels unstable — to believe that His presence is your protection and His Word your assurance.

This is what the secret place becomes: not an escape from the world, but an anchoring in God that allows you to stand in the world without losing your peace. The Father meets you there. Not occasionally — consistently. Not reluctantly — eagerly.

Reflection

Have I been visiting God or abiding in Him?

Have I allowed my relationship with the Father to be shaped by routine, or by intimacy?

How is the Holy Spirit inviting me deeper into the secret place in this season?

Prayer

Father, thank You for calling me into the secret place — into abiding intimacy with You. Teach me to silence the noise and slow down long enough to enjoy Your presence. Help me trust Your heart so deeply that prayer becomes not an obligation but a refuge. Draw me into lingering, listening, and loving communion with You. Let abiding in Your presence become the rhythm of my life. In Jesus' name, Amen.

THE JOURNEY CONTINUES:

There comes a point in the journey when the secret place is no longer just a moment you visit — it becomes a home your heart cannot live without. When you have tasted what happens there... when you have felt the nearness of God settle every anxious corner of your soul... when you have learned to breathe again in His presence... something in you begins to crave consistency.

Because even encounters need foundations.

The secret place awakens hunger, but it is **a place of prayer** that sustains it. Encounters introduce you to God's presence, but consistency establishes His presence in you. The moments when heaven feels close are never meant to be rare accidents — they are invitations into rhythm, into habit, into relationship.

From the beginning, God has always worked through **place**.

Creation had order because everything had a place. Redemption was secured because Jesus took our place. Eternity is promised because He has prepared a place. And prayer becomes transformation when **you give God a place** — not a leftover moment, not scattered attention, but a chosen space in your life that belongs to Him.

The secret place shows you what your heart was made for.

But the **purpose and importance of a place** teaches your heart to return — again and again — until His presence becomes the environment you live from, not just the moment you seek.

And that is where the next chapter leads.

The Purpose and Importance of a Place — why where you meet with God matters just as much as that you meet with Him.

THE PURPOSE AND IMPORTANCE OF A "PLACE"

Have you ever noticed that God never creates anything without giving it a place? Before the first sunrise ever broke across creation, God arranged everything with intention. The sun had its place. The moon had hers. The sea stayed within the boundaries He assigned, and the stars shined exactly where He set them (Genesis 1). Nothing God made was left to drift.

And then... He formed humanity.

But unlike anything else, He didn't just give us a place — He gave us a place **with Him**. The garden wasn't just a beautiful setting. It was a sanctuary of presence — the first secret place. A home where love flowed freely, where identity wasn't earned but received, where belonging was never questioned.

You were created for that kind of place — a place where your soul knows, *"I'm home."*

Jesus understood how deeply we wrestle with belonging. That's why He said something so tender, so personal, that it still reaches inside every heart that has ever felt alone: "I go to prepare a place for you" (John 14:2). Not a general space. Not a crowded room. A prepared place — with your name on it. Jesus wasn't only speaking of eternity someday — He was speaking to the longing inside you **right now**.

Because God has always been the God of place.

But place is not only geographical. It is spiritual. Emotional. Eternal. And the decisions we make in time shape the place we will occupy forever. Scripture makes a sobering statement about Judas: "...that he might go to his own place" (Acts 1:25). His choices led him somewhere God never intended him to live. That one sentence reminds us — time matters. Trust matters. Surrender matters. Because place matters.

Right now, in this very moment, Jesus is knocking on the door of your heart. "Behold, I stand at the door and knock" (Revelation 3:20). That invitation is not only about heaven in the future — it is about His presence right now. The One preparing a place for you in eternity is asking for a place in you today.

Every day, you decide who will occupy the chambers of your heart. Jesus enters by invitation. The enemy enters through neglect. One brings peace. The other brings pressure. One leads you to rest. The other drives you into fear.

Your heart was never designed to stay empty. It was designed to host presence.

That is why Scripture warns, "Neither give place to the devil" (Ephesians 4:27). Every part of your life that isn't surrendered to God becomes open territory to darkness. Surrender isn't just a moment — it's a lifestyle. A continual welcoming of the Father into every corner of who you are. The more space you give Him, the more His presence transforms you.

And when the Father enters, He doesn't simply take a seat — He begins rebuilding the home He intends to occupy. He removes what cannot carry His glory. He heals wounds you've learned to function with. He touches attitudes and patterns that quietly war against peace. He restores what was damaged so that you can hold what He desires to pour into you.

He makes His home... holy.

Adam and Eve knew God as Creator — but not yet as Father. He walked with them in the cool of the day (Genesis 3:8), but He did not dwell within them. We live on the other side of redemption. Calvary changed the relationship. What humanity once lost through sin has been restored through Christ. God's presence doesn't visit anymore — it abides. The Holy Spirit has moved into the very place Jesus died to prepare — **you**.

We invite Him not because we are strong — but because we have tasted emptiness... and we never want to go back.

But even a sacred place must be guarded. Distraction can invade. Fear can intrude. The noise of life can crowd out the nearness you were created to enjoy. That's why Jesus taught us to pray in the secret place with the door shut (Matthew 6:6) — not just the physical door of a room, but the inner doors labeled anxiety, hurry, and divided affection. You cannot hear His whisper while the world is shouting.

Closing the door is trust. It is choosing Him above everything else in that moment. It is saying, *"Father, this time and this space belong to You."*

And when that inner door shuts... heaven opens.

Strength comes where weakness lived. Clarity replaces confusion. Faith pushes out fear. The world may never witness what happens there — but the world will witness the results. You carry the atmosphere of where you dwell. People may not be able to explain it, but they will sense it — the calm, the patience, the peace — the fragrance of the Father.

This is the purpose of a place — to give God a home in you, and to give you a home in Him. The One preparing a place for you in eternity is longing for a prepared place in you today. With every moment of surrender, you give Him more room to dwell — and more room to transform.

THE JOURNEY CONTINUES

Having a place of prayer matters because it trains the heart to return. It builds a rhythm — not of religion, but of relationship. When you keep showing up in the same place to meet with God, something begins to change inside you. The place becomes familiar... and so does His presence. Your spirit starts to recognize the atmosphere where you've prayed before, wept before, listened before, and been strengthened before.

But once you have a place, there comes a moment when God invites you into something deeper.

It is no longer just about going **to** the place — it becomes about slowing down **in** the place.

The heart begins to quiet. The mind unclenches. The emotions settle their frantic pace. The soul grows still enough to notice Him.

That is where prayer turns into communion.

That is where listening becomes just as sacred as speaking.

And that is where the next chapter unfolds:

The Stillness 'That Speaks: Learning to Listen in Prayer.'

CHAPTER 4

THE STILLNESS THAT SPEAKS: LEARNING TO LISTEN IN PRAYER

I've learned something over the years—some of the most sacred moments with God happen when everything becomes still and quiet. Not just when the TV is off or the phone is set aside, but when the noise inside of you finally settles.

It's that deep peace that calms the storm in your soul and reminds you that God has been near the whole time.

For years, I thought prayer was all about words. I believed the more I said, the more spiritual I must be. Maybe you've felt something similar—that if you're not talking, you're not really praying.

But the Holy Spirit began to teach me something much deeper: real prayer is not measured by how much you speak; it's measured by how much you hear.

When you learn to wait in God's presence—without rushing, without trying to force an answer—something begins to shift inside. Your mind slows down. Your heart softens. You start to sense His nearness. You realize He has been speaking all along; you just needed to become still enough to listen.

THE WHISPER THAT REVEALS HIS HEART

I remember a young woman in our church who came to see me one day, clearly frustrated and tired.

"Pastor," she said, "I pray and pray, but I never hear anything. I feel like God is silent."

I smiled gently and said, "Sometimes God's silence is not His absence—it's His invitation."

She looked puzzled, so I continued, "He may be teaching you to stop chasing His answers and start resting in His presence. When you learn to rest, you'll start recognizing His whisper."

We prayed together, and then I gave her a simple assignment for the next seven days.

"No long lists," I told her. "No striving. Don't try to impress God with your words. For one week, sit in His presence and ask for nothing. Let your heart listen."

A week later, she came back with tears in her eyes.

"Something changed," she said quietly. "The first couple of days felt awkward. I didn't know what to say—or not say. But by the third day, I started to notice a peace I can't explain. Scriptures I had read years ago began to come back to my mind. I felt like God was reminding me, 'I'm here. I haven't left you.'"

She paused, then added, "I realized He had been speaking—I was just too busy filling the silence."

That is the beauty of listening prayer. God has not stopped speaking. He is still guiding, still comforting, still correcting, still revealing. But He will not compete with the constant noise. His voice is not usually in the shouting; it's in the whisper.

And in that whisper, He reveals His heart.

If it seems like God has been silent in your life, it may not be that He is far away. It may be that He is whispering—inviting you to draw closer than you've ever been.

THE BEAUTY OF HOLY QUIETNESS

Stillness is not weakness, and it is not laziness. Stillness is choosing to become quiet before God so you can hear Him clearly.

Elijah learned this in one of the lowest moments of his life.

The prophet was tired, afraid, and hiding in a cave on Mount Horeb. He felt alone. He felt finished. He had just come from a great victory on Mount Carmel, but now he was exhausted and ready to give up.

Then God told him to stand on the mountain.

A powerful wind came and tore into the mountains, breaking rocks in pieces—but God was not in the wind.

Then an earthquake shook the ground—but God was not in the earthquake.

After that came a fire—but God was not in the fire either.

Then came a still, small voice. A gentle whisper.

And in that whisper, God spoke to Elijah (see 1 Kings 19:11–13).

The whisper was personal. It wasn't God showing off His power; it was God revealing His closeness. He didn't shout to prove that He was God. He whispered to pull Elijah nearer.

God often uses stillness because stillness requires you to lean in.

When someone whispers, you can't stay distant. You have to move closer to hear them. That is what true prayer is—leaning in to hear His heart.

So if it seems like God has been quiet in your life, it may not be that He is far away. It may be that He is whispering—calling you closer, inviting you into a deeper level of trust and intimacy.

JESUS AND THE EARLY MORNING STILLNESS

Jesus modeled this life of quiet communion with the Father.

Luke 5:16 tells us, "But Jesus often withdrew to lonely places and prayed."

Before the crowds gathered.

Before the sick reached for His touch.

Before demons were cast out and miracles unfolded—

Jesus stepped away to be alone with His Father.

He did not just speak to the Father; He listened with the Father. His public authority flowed out of His private intimacy.

Those early hours were more than a "prayer time"; they were heart-to-heart time. In that quiet, He received direction. In that stillness, He found strength for the cross that lay ahead.

If Jesus, the Son of God, needed stillness, you and I certainly do.

If He needed to withdraw, to step away from the noise, to sit alone with the Father and listen, then we should not be surprised when the Holy Spirit calls us into the same pattern.

Stillness does not make you less effective—it makes you more aligned. It clears the fog so you can see what the Father is doing and agree with it.

Learning to listen in prayer is not a luxury for "deep" Christians. It is essential for every believer who wants to walk in clarity and power.

THE MIRACLE OF STILLNESS

I once heard about a pastor who went to see a man in the hospital who had slipped into a coma. The man's wife sat by his bed, worn out from days of prayer and tears.

"Pastor," she said softly, "I've run out of words."

After many years of meeting God in quiet moments, that pastor had learned the power of simple presence. He took her hand and said gently, "Then don't say another word. Let's just sit in His presence."

They did.

For several minutes, they said nothing. No long prayers. No emotional speeches. They simply worshiped quietly in their hearts, turned their attention toward God, and waited.

After a while, the pastor sensed the Holy Spirit nudge his heart: "Sing."

Softly, he began to sing, "Great Is Thy Faithfulness."

As he sang, the man's fingers twitched. His wife gasped and began to weep. The pastor kept singing. Moments later, the man's eyes opened. He could not speak yet, but a single tear rolled down his cheek.

Over the next few weeks, the man slowly recovered. Eventually, the doctors discharged him from the hospital.

It wasn't the length or volume of their prayer that moved heaven. It was the stillness that made room for God to move.

Stories like this simply confirm what Scripture has already shown us: stillness can become the stage where God does some of His greatest work.

THE FRUIT OF A LISTENING HEART

People who spend time in stillness with God carry something different about them.

They don't rush like everyone else.

They move with purpose.

They may speak fewer words, but their words carry the weight of heaven.

You can tell when someone has been alone with God. There is a calm strength, a steady peace, a quiet confidence that does not come from personality—it comes from presence.

When you become a listener, your decisions become clearer. Your heart becomes calmer. Your prayer life goes deeper. You begin to realize that prayer was never about trying to get God to notice you. It was always about giving Him your full attention.

Moses came down from Mount Sinai with his face shining because he had spent time in God's presence (see Exodus 34:29). That is what happens when you learn to listen. His light begins to show on your life.

You may not see a physical glow in the mirror, but others will notice something different. They may not be able to explain it, but they will feel it—a peace that doesn't make sense, a wisdom that seems beyond your years, a love that does not come from human effort.

Listening makes room for the Holy Spirit to shape your responses, soften your words, and guide your choices. Instead of reacting from pressure, you respond from a place of peace.

HOW TO CULTIVATE STILLNESS

Stillness doesn't just "happen." In a noisy world, you have to choose it on purpose. Let me give you a few simple ways to begin this practice:

1. Designate a sacred space.

Choose a quiet corner, a chair, a spot on the porch, or a room where you sense peace. It doesn't have to be fancy. Consistency turns ordinary places into altars.

2. Begin with gratitude.

Start by thanking Him for who He is before you ask for what you need. Gratitude softens the heart and opens the door to His presence.

3. Read a verse slowly.

Take a short passage of Scripture and read it slowly, more than once. Let the Word settle in your spirit like rain soaking into dry ground. Ask the Holy Spirit, "What are You saying to me through this?"

4. Wait in silence.

This may be the hardest part at first. Don't rush to fill the space. God speaks in rhythm, not in haste. Let the silence stretch longer than feels comfortable, and trust that He is working in the quiet.

5. Write what you sense.

Keep a simple journal. Jot down impressions, scriptures, names, or thoughts that come to mind as you wait before Him. Over time, you'll begin to see patterns—ways He has been guiding you all along.

Stillness doesn't mean doing nothing—it means making room for God.

In a world that constantly pulls at your attention, stillness is how you push back and say, "My heart belongs to Him first."

You may not always feel something dramatic in those moments. Some days will feel ordinary. But every time you choose to be still before God, you are training your heart to listen, and you are building a history with Him.

Listening prayer is not about earning revelation; it is about living aware of His presence.

REFLECTION QUESTIONS

When you think about prayer, do you naturally focus more on speaking or on listening? Why do you think that is?

Where in your daily routine could you intentionally create a few minutes of stillness before God?

Have there been times when you later realized God was speaking, but you were too busy or anxious to notice? What can you learn from those moments?

What fears or distractions make stillness difficult for you, and how is the Holy Spirit inviting you to surrender them?

PRAYER

Father, teach me the beauty of holy stillness.

Quiet the noise in my mind so I can hear the whispers of Your Spirit. Help me to stop chasing constant activity and learn to rest in Your presence. When it feels like nothing is happening, remind me that You are still working in the quiet.

Train my heart to listen. Show me how to wait in faith, to trust in silence, and to rest in Your love. Let Your peace be my teacher and Your presence my home. Speak to me, even in the stillness—and when You speak, help me to obey.

In Jesus' name, Amen.

COMING NEXT

The more you sit in stillness before God, the more you begin to understand something the disciples saw in Jesus.

They did not just watch Him preach to crowds or perform miracles—they watched Him withdraw. They watched Him rise early, slip away to quiet places, and return carrying a peace and power that could not be explained by human effort. Somewhere in those moments of listening, a realization dawned in their hearts:

Whatever He has with the Father... we need that too.

They had been raised on prayers. They knew the words. They knew the customs. But what they saw in Jesus was different. His prayers were not empty recitations; they were living conversations. His time with the Father left a mark on everything He did.

Eventually, they could not hold back the cry inside them any longer. One day, as He finished praying, they finally said what their hearts had been whispering for a long time:

"Lord, teach us to pray."

That same cry is rising in you.

You have learned to adore.

You have learned to draw near to the secret place.

You are beginning to value the stillness that speaks.

Now it is time to let the Holy Spirit lead you into the same school of prayer that shaped the disciples—where Jesus Himself becomes your Teacher.

Next, we step into that honest request and the answer that still shapes every believer's prayer life in:

Lord, Teach Us to Pray: The Heart of the Disciples' Cry

CHAPTER 5

LORD, TEACH US TO PRAY: THE HEART BEHIND THE CRY

The disciples had watched Jesus heal the sick, open blind eyes, and command raging storms into stillness. They had heard His words—every sentence saturated with grace and carried with authority. Yet, for all they had seen and heard, it was not the miracles that stirred their deepest longing.

It was His prayer life.

They had grown up reciting prayers steeped in tradition. From childhood, they were taught the words, the forms, and the patterns of Jewish prayer. But what they witnessed in Jesus was unlike anything they had ever known. He prayed with intimacy, not just formality—with a nearness to the Father that released divine power and undeniable results.

At some point, they realized something profound:
They had been taught **how** to pray, but they had never known how **Jesus** prayed.

In this chapter, we will explore the heart behind their humble request—their earnest cry that still echoes through every generation of believers:

"Lord, teach us to pray."

THE MOST POWERFUL REQUEST THE DISCIPLES EVER MADE

I often wonder what it must have been like to stand among the disciples and watch Jesus pray.

They had seen Him teach multitudes with wisdom no one could refute. They had watched Him lay hands on the sick and see them recover. They had heard Him speak to storms, and nature itself obeyed.

Yet, those things—miraculous as they were—were not what stirred their deepest curiosity.

It was His **communion** with the Father.

There was something different about the way He prayed. It wasn't the length of His prayers or the eloquence of His words. It was the intimacy of His tone. He spoke to God not as a distant Sovereign seated in unreachable glory, but as a Son speaking to His Father.

Every Jewish boy learned to pray. By the time a young man reached his Bar Mitzvah at about thirteen, he was considered a "son of the law." He knew the rhythm of Jewish prayer—the posture, the pauses, the repetitions.

But what they heard in Jesus was unlike any rabbi they had ever known.

When He prayed, heaven did not feel far away—it felt near.

His words carried an authority that did not come from rigid ritual, but from real relationship. He addressed God as **Abba**.

That single word shattered centuries of distance.

It was not a formal title; it was an intimate whisper. Abba was the word a small child would use as he ran into his father's arms. It meant "Papa," "Daddy"—a word full of tenderness, safety, and trust.

The disciples had heard rabbis pray to **Elohim**, the Almighty Creator, and to **Adonai**, the Sovereign Lord—but **Abba**? That was different.

That was personal.

That was family.

I can almost see Peter watching Him, arms folded, brow furrowed in thought. John, the youngest, leaning in a little closer, eyes wide with wonder. Perhaps Matthew, once a despised tax collector, felt something awakening inside—a dawning realization that love like this might even include him.

They had stood near the presence of power.

But now they were witnessing the power of **presence**.

THE CRY THAT CHANGED EVERYTHING

One day, after watching Jesus withdraw yet again to a solitary place and return with that same deep peace and unshakeable authority, one of them finally voiced what they were all feeling:

"Lord, teach us to pray" (Luke 11:1).

It was not the voice of a scholar asking for a new technique.

It was the voice of a son longing for relationship.

They were not simply asking Him to teach them **how** to pray.

They were asking Him to teach them **to pray**.

There is a difference.

Teaching someone **how** to pray focuses on words, posture, and discipline. It can cover structure, patterns, and timing.

Teaching someone **to** pray deals with desire, hunger, and the heart. It awakens longing. It stirs love. It draws you into relationship.

The first can be learned through instruction.

The second can only be awakened through encounter.

When they made that request, it was not because they knew nothing about prayer. It was because they knew their current experience was not enough. They had memorized prayers, but they had not yet entered the kind of fellowship they saw in Jesus.

They had learned the language of prayer.
Now they wanted to learn the **life** of prayer.

I understand that longing. I have prayed prayers that sounded right but felt empty. I have quoted promises that I believed, yet my heart still felt dry. And like the disciples, I have found myself whispering, "Lord, teach me to pray—not to perform, but to connect. Not just to repeat, but to **relate**."

That is the heart behind the disciples' cry.

WHEN PRAYER MOVES FROM FORMULA TO FELLOWSHIP

Jesus did not respond to their request with a rebuke. He answered with revelation.

He did not begin by correcting their posture or critiquing their phrasing. He began by revealing relationship.

"When you pray, say:
'Our Father in heaven,
Hallowed be Your name...'" (Luke 11:2, NKJV).

Before Jesus taught them **what** to say, He taught them **whom** they were talking to.

Notice this: He did not say, "When I pray, I say, My Father."
Instead, He opened the door and said, "When **you** pray, say: **Our Father**."

In that one phrase, He invited them into the same intimacy He shared with God Himself. He opened a door that religion had kept closed—the door to **sonship**.

He was saying, in essence:

"You are not outsiders trying to earn access.

You are sons and daughters with a standing invitation."

From that moment forward, prayer was redefined.

It was no longer about trying to earn an audience.

It became about enjoying a relationship.

I remember the first time that truth truly settled into my own spirit.

I was sitting alone after a long day of ministry. My prayers had become mechanical—lists, requests, intercessions. All of it was good, but somewhere along the way, the joy had faded. I was still praying, but my heart was tired.

In that quiet, I sensed the Lord whisper to my heart:

"Stop talking to Me like I'm far away."

The words startled me. I stopped mid-sentence.

Then I sensed Him say,

"I'm not on the other side of your prayers—I'm here."

It felt as though the atmosphere shifted in the room. His nearness was no longer a concept—it was a reality. Not doctrine, but presence. In that moment, I understood more deeply what Jesus was showing His disciples.

Prayer was never meant to bridge an impossible distance.

In Christ, the distance has already been removed.

INTIMACY BEFORE INTERCESSION

When you begin prayer with "Our Father," something shifts inside you.

Your posture changes. Fear softens into faith. Anxiety moves aside for assurance. Performance yields to peace. You stop trying to convince God to listen, and you start resting in the truth that He already knows and loves you.

This is why Jesus began with adoration before moving to petition:

"Hallowed be Your name."

He was teaching them that before we ask God for anything; we acknowledge who He is.

Adoration anchors the heart before intercession engages the hand.

Too often, we rush into prayer with a list in our hands and worry in our hearts. We pour out needs and crises before ever lifting our eyes.

But when you start prayer by worshiping—by remembering that He is holy, faithful, present, powerful—your heart begins to settle. Your priorities re-align. Your needs are still real, but they no longer feel like the center of everything. God does.

Adoration aligns you with heaven's rhythm. It quiets anxiety and stirs awareness.

When you begin prayer by beholding the Father, your spirit remembers:

This is not a negotiation.

This is communion.

THE SECRET OF JESUS' AUTHORITY

The disciples never asked Jesus, "Teach us to preach."

They never said, "Teach us how to work miracles."

They said, "Lord, teach us to pray."

Why?

Because they eventually realized that **everything else flowed from there**.

They had seen Him walk into demon-filled situations with unflinching peace.

They had watched storms obey His voice, sickness flee at His word, and bread multiply in His hands.

But they also noticed a pattern:

Every public demonstration of power was preceded by private fellowship in prayer.

Luke 5:16 tells us, "So He Himself often withdrew into the wilderness and prayed."

The wilderness was not His punishment—it was His preparation.

It was there, in quiet places and hidden moments, that He aligned Himself with the Father's will, listened for heaven's instruction, and carried that instruction back into a broken world.

If the Son of God needed that rhythm of retreat and return, how much more do we?

I have learned this the hard way:
The strength of your public life will never exceed the depth of your private life.

Ministry becomes heavy when prayer becomes hollow.
We burn out when we pour out without first being filled.

Jesus' authority flowed from intimacy.
Ours will too.

THE TRANSFORMATION OF THE HEART

The purpose of prayer was never to change God's mind.
The purpose of prayer is to change ours.

When you kneel in the secret place, something shifts inside you.

Fear begins to loosen its grip.
Pride melts in His presence.
Self-reliance gives way to surrender.

You pray less from your raw emotions and more from His Spirit.
You stop only praying *to* God and begin praying *with* God.

Romans 8:26 tells us, "The Spirit Himself makes intercession for us with groanings which cannot be uttered."

Prayer becomes partnership.

The Holy Spirit joins your weakness with His wisdom, your groans with His grace. You bring the vessel, and He fills it. You bring the words, and He breathes on them.

And through that communion, transformation happens—not only around you, but **within** you.

I have seen this in my own life. In seasons when I was most broken, most weary, most uncertain—those were the moments when prayer reshaped me the most. Sometimes, it did not change my circumstances overnight. But it always changed **me**.

It taught me to wait without collapsing, to trust without proof, and to love without conditions.

That is the miracle of intimacy:

It matures you.

WHEN HEAVEN MEETS THE HUMAN HEART

The disciples came to understand that prayer was not limited to "holy" times or certain locations.

Jesus prayed on mountaintops, in gardens, at tables, and even on the cross.

He showed them that prayer is not an event—it is a lifestyle. It is the continual awareness of the Father's presence in every moment.

When you live that way, ordinary spaces become sacred.

The drive to work becomes an altar.

The kitchen sink becomes a sanctuary.

The silent sigh before a difficult conversation becomes an act of surrender.

Prayer stops being something you schedule and becomes part of who you are.

When heaven meets the human heart like that, everything becomes holy ground.

WHEN THE SILENCE TEACHES

There must have been times when the disciples wondered why Jesus stayed in prayer so long.

The early hours before dawn.

The moments before major decisions.

The solitude after great miracles.

All filled with stillness.

Silence is not the absence of God's voice.

Often, it is the place where His voice is amplified.

In stillness, you begin to hear what hurry has been drowning out.

When I first began to practice listening instead of leading every moment of the conversation, it felt awkward. My thoughts raced. My mind wandered. I kept feeling the urge to "do" something—say more, ask more, move on.

But as I remained, something changed.

The inner noise started to quiet down. And in that quiet, a different kind of knowing emerged—not from long sentences, but from His presence.

Silence became my teacher.

In that silence, the Lord exposed fears I had buried and wounds I had ignored. He reminded me that He loved me before I ever preached a sermon or prayed what I thought was a "perfect" prayer.

The disciples discovered that as well. When they asked Him, "Lord, teach us to pray," they were not just learning words. They were learning **rhythm**—the rhythm of rest, response, and revelation.

THE SCHOOL OF PRAYER

Prayer is the school where God shapes His sons and daughters.

It is where we learn to see from His perspective and speak from His authority.

Right after giving them the pattern we call the Lord's Prayer, Jesus told a parable (Luke 11:5–10). He spoke of a man who went to his friend at midnight, asking for bread to feed an unexpected guest. At first, the friend resisted—his door was shut; his family was already in bed. But because of the man's persistence, the friend eventually got up and gave him what he needed.

Jesus was not teaching us how to manipulate God.

He was teaching us how to trust Him.

"Keep asking. Keep seeking. Keep knocking."

Persistence in prayer does not overcome God's reluctance.

It proves our dependence.

Prayer trains the heart to trust beyond what the eyes can see.

When we keep coming to Him, we are saying,

"Father, I still believe You are good.

I still believe You hear me.

I still believe Your timing is perfect—even when I do not understand it."

Through that persistence, our faith is refined.

FROM INTIMACY TO IMPACT

True prayer always leads to transformation.

And true transformation always leads to impact.

When you have been with the Father, people can tell.

Moses' face shone after he met with God.

Stephen's face radiated with glory even as stones were being hurled at him.

Jesus' garments glistened with a heavenly light on the Mount of Transfiguration.

You cannot hide the residue of His presence.

It is the difference between speaking **about** God and speaking **from** God.

Between quoting Scripture and carrying revelation.

Between performing ministry and releasing life.

The disciples themselves were changed after Pentecost. The same men who once hid in fear stood boldly before rulers and proclaimed the gospel with power. Scripture says the people around them "realized that they had been with Jesus" (Acts 4:13, NIV).

That is the fruit of a heart that has truly learned to pray.

When you know the Father, you begin to reflect Him.

When you commune with heaven, you begin to carry it.

THE ABBA REVELATION

The deeper you go in prayer, the clearer one truth becomes:

Everything begins with **Abba**.

You will never pray with confidence until you see God as Father.

Not distant.

Not disinterested.

Not unpredictable or easily displeased.

A Father.

This is one reason the enemy fights so fiercely to damage the image of fatherhood in our world. If he can distort your understanding of what a father is, he can damage your ability to trust the Father's heart. A wounded heart often struggles to believe—even when the One reaching for it is good.

But when the revelation of Abba reaches your soul, everything changes in prayer.

Prayer stops feeling like a performance.

You stop trying to impress Him.

You stop approaching Him like a servant begging for mercy, and you start approaching Him like a child who belongs at the table.

You finally begin to understand:

You are not trying to get God's attention.

You already have it.

When that truth sinks in, prayer becomes a joy instead of a burden.

A connection instead of a chore.

A meeting of hearts instead of a mere list of requests.

This is the cry behind every sincere prayer:

"Lord, teach us to pray."

Not because we do not know the words,

but because we long to know the Father.

That is not just a request from long ago.

It is the echo of every believer's heart.

We all come to moments when words fail, strength fades, and nothing seems to work but prayer. And in those moments, we rediscover what the disciples discovered—that prayer is not a skill to master, but a relationship to nurture.

God does not need polished phrases. He wants honest hearts.

He does not respond to performance. He responds to **presence**.

When you finally surrender your need to be impressive, you will discover His invitation to be intimate.

That is when prayer truly comes alive.

REFLECTION QUESTIONS

What does calling God "Abba" stir within you? Does it challenge your view of Him or comfort it? Why?

Have your prayers become more about routine than relationship? What would it look like to return to intimacy in this season?

Where have you been persistent in prayer, and how might God be using that persistence to shape your faith?

In what ways might God be using **silence** right now—not to punish you, but to deepen your trust and teach you to listen?

PRAYER

Father, thank You for calling me closer.

Teach me to pray—not just with my lips, but with my life. Let my words flow out of intimacy, not obligation. Reveal Yourself to me as Abba—the One who sees me, loves me, and delights to be with me.

When I grow weary, remind me that prayer is not my effort to reach You—it is Your invitation for me to rest in You. Let my heart echo the cry of the disciples: "Lord, teach me to pray."

Shape my life until every thought, every breath, and every moment becomes communion with You.

In Jesus' name, Amen.

COMING NEXT

Learning to pray is not only about your words. It is also about your **heart**. Jesus made it clear that the Father is not impressed with performance; He is moved by sincerity, humility, and truth.

Prayer from the lips can sound right.

Prayer from the heart reaches heaven.

In the next chapter, we will step into the place where true connection begins—where God is not just listening to what you say, but looking at the altar inside you.

Next: God Wants Your Heart, Not Your Performance.

CHAPTER 6

GOD WANTS YOUR HEART, NOT YOUR PERFORMANCE

My wife and I were in New York, attending a church where I had been invited as one of the keynote speakers. Several pastors were also scheduled to preach—one was well-known in the area, and another possessed a rare combination of vocal talent and eloquence that captivated audiences with ease. The atmosphere throughout the services was electric—filled with excitement, noise, and movement. Yet, beneath all that energy, something vital was missing: His Presence.

When it came time for me to minister, the Holy Spirit prompted me to do something unexpected. Instead of matching the energy of the moment, He led me to guide the congregation into a quiet, reverent flow—a holy hush that invited stillness before God. As the music softened and the noise faded, hearts began to quiet. You could sense the shift in the room—the atmosphere that once pulsed with performance became heavy with Presence.

It was in that stillness that the Lord began to move—not through noise or applause, but through tears, whispers, and awe. The same people who moments earlier were spectators became worshippers, overcome not by emotion, but by encounter.

As I ministered, the presence of the Lord filled the church like a gentle wave, rolling through every heart in the room. When I gave the altar call—for the lost, the hurting, and the hungry—the people came flooding forward. You could feel heaven drawing them. That night became a divine exchange—salvation for the sinner, deliverance for the bound, healing for the broken, and restoration for the weary.

After the service, the pastor asked to speak with me privately. The sanctuary had grown quiet now, the lights dimmed, with the lingering fragrance of worship still hanging softly in the air. He looked at me for a long moment, his expression thoughtful, and said, "I watched how you prayed tonight. There was no performance, no flair—just a simplicity that carried weight. Yet as you prayed, the presence of God filled the entire sanctuary. I saw my people—some with tears in their eyes—not just listening, but praying with you. Not loudly, not for attention, but reverently. It was as though heaven came near."

Then he began to speak about the message I had preached—"You Received Jesus as Savior, But Have You Made Him Lord in Your Life?"

He said softly, "That message didn't just move me—it convicted me. It opened my eyes and made me question how much of my own life I've truly surrendered to Christ's Lordship. And it wasn't just me. When you made the altar call, I saw some of my elders praying and weeping. Even some of my men—those who never show emotion—came to me afterward saying their entire perspective on their relationship with Jesus had changed."

He paused, then smiled and shook his head, still in awe. As we continued talking, his secretary quietly entered the room and handed him a receipt. He glanced at it casually—then did a double take. "What... are you sure?" he asked, looking up in surprise. She nodded, smiling in disbelief. "Yes, Pastor. I double-checked it twice," she said softly before slipping out of the room.

He sat there for a moment, staring at the paper in his hand, slowly shaking his head as though trying to take it all in. Then he looked up at me, eyes wide with astonishment, and said, "Dr. Simpson, of the three nights of services, we received the largest offering *tonight*—after you ministered. It's more than double what was received in the previous two nights."

He leaned back, still visibly moved. "And what amazes me most," he continued, "is that you never pushed or pleaded for it. You simply spoke with such grace and faith that people wanted to give.

Leaning back, he looked at me thoughtfully. "Tell me, Dr. Simpson," he said, his tone earnest, "what is your secret? You don't whoop, you don't sing, yet there's such a powerful anointing that rests on you. It's in your prayers, your preaching—even in the way you receive the offering. The way you move in the gifts of the Spirit feels so natural, so effortless. You flow with such grace that it pulls people in—not toward you, but toward God. I'm serious—what's your secret? There's something different about the way you minister."

His sincerity humbled me. I looked at him and said, "My friend, it's not performance—it's presence. Any success I've had in ministry is tied to my prayer life. Just as the key to Jesus' power was His intimacy with the Father, so it is with us. If you want a greater anointing, spend time daily at the altar with the One who anoints. The oil only flows where there is surrender. Every encounter in His presence leaves a residue of power; every moment of intimacy births fresh authority. The secret to carrying the anointing is not found in striving—it's found in staying. Stay at the altar, and the fragrance of His presence will go with you wherever you go."

The pastor looked puzzled for a moment. "Are you saying I need to come to church and get on the altar every day?" he asked, clearly sincere, already imagining how to make it possible.

I smiled and placed a hand on his shoulder. "No, my friend," I said warmly. "Your heart is the altar. That's where true prayers rise before God. You know what the altar represents—it's the place of sacrifice, surrender, and submission. It's where you lay down your will so that God's will can be done. When your heart becomes that altar—when it's fully yielded before Him—heaven always responds."

He sat quietly for a moment, eyes glistening, the truth sinking deep. The sanctuary was still, as though the very air had paused to listen. It wasn't just another conversation—it was a divine moment, a life-changing moment.

"Prayer, like worship, must come from the heart." I told him. "When your heart communes with God," I continued... "His presence flows through everything you do—your words, your prayers, even the atmosphere around you."

He nodded, tears in his eyes. Then, I joined hands with him and prayed. As we prayed; the presence of God filled the room. We both trembled as His power surged through us—heaven's approval resting on that moment. The air grew thick with glory; worship became adoration. When the Spirit lifted, I gave him counsel on fasting and learning to yield to the Holy Ghost.

God Wants Your Heart, Not Your Performance

You've walked with me through a truth that changes everything—God isn't after your performance; He's after your heart. Somewhere along the way, religion taught us to labor to impress Him, but relationship teaches us to invite Him. It's not the length of your prayers or the beauty of your words that moves His heart—it's the honesty and intent behind them.

If you've been feeling weary, trying to pray the "right" way, pause for a moment. The Father never asked you to be perfect in prayer; He asked you to be real. Every sigh, every tear, every whispered word from a sincere heart is sacred to Him. That's where true connection begins—in the quiet surrender of being fully known and still completely loved.

So before we step into what's next, let your heart breathe. You don't have to strive to reach Him—He's already near. Let your heart settle in that truth for a moment. Feel the weight lift as His presence meets you right where you are.

Reflection

Have I been trying to reach God through effort instead of relationship?

What might shift in my prayer life if I simply showed up with my whole heart?

Have I made Jesus not only my Savior, but also the Lord of my life?

Prayer

Father, I'm learning that You're not looking for perfection—You're looking for me. Teach me to bring my heart, not my performance. Strip away the pressure to sound right, and fill me with the freedom to be real in Your presence. Help me to make Jesus not only my Savior, but also the Lord of my life. Let my heart become the place where Your Spirit rests and my soul finds peace. In Jesus' name, Amen.

It's About The Heart

When you finally stop trying to earn His approval and start offering Him your heart, something shifts. That's where transformation begins. That's where worship turns into communion, and prayer becomes more than words—it becomes life.

Because prayer doesn't truly begin on your lips—it begins on the altar of your heart. And that's where we're going next.

Your Heart: The Altar Where True Prayer Begins.

CHAPTER 7

YOUR HEART, THE ALTAR WHERE TRUE PRAYER BEGINS

Years ago, I counseled a man who had walked away from ministry after a deep moral failure. He sat across from me, shoulders slumped beneath the weight of shame, eyes downcast, the air thick with regret. After a long silence, he finally said softly, "Pastor, I can't even pray anymore. I feel too far gone. I don't believe that there is any hope for me."

I looked at him gently and asked, "Then why are you here?"

He hesitated, staring at the floor before answering softly, "Honestly, I don't know."

Leaning forward, I said, "You may not know—but your spirit does. The voice of condemnation is shouting so loudly in your mind that you can't hear the voice of the Spirit calling you back to the altar. You're here because your heart heard God's call. That's why you reached out."

Tears welled in his eyes as the truth sank in. I could feel the atmosphere shift—heaven drawing near to reclaim what shame had tried to silence.

You don't need the perfect words," I said gently. "Just turn your heart toward Him in repentance. God never walked away from the altar—He's been waiting for you there. Speak to Him from the depth of your heart.

He looked up and said, "Lord, please forgive me. I am so sorry for failing

You—for hurting You and others."

We sat quietly for a moment before I led him in prayer. As we prayed, the presence of God filled the office where we were sitting. His trembling words gave way to weeping, and his weeping turned into worship.

The same man who earlier had said he couldn't pray was now pouring out his heart before the One who had never stopped loving him.

Time seemed to stand still. No clock could measure what heaven was doing in that room. As he wept, years of guilt melted away beneath the power of grace. The heaviness that had chained his soul lifted, replaced by the unmistakable peace of God's presence.

Later, he shared with a voice of praise. "I feel... free...the pain, guilt, and shame is gone!"

I smiled, and said. "That's what happens when grace meets surrender. The altar isn't a place of punishment—it's a place of exchange. You came carrying guilt and shame, but you're leaving clothed in love and grace."

He sat back, with a big smile of gratitude on his face and visibly transformed. His countenance was lighter, his eyes clear, his spirit free. "Pastor," he said softly, "I thought God was done with me. But now I know He's not."

I nodded. "God doesn't discard vessels that have been cracked—He restores them for greater use. God can repurpose the very failure the enemy meant to destroy you with and use it to help others overcome theirs—just as Jesus did with Peter when He said, *'And when you return to Me, Peter, strengthen your brothers.' (Luke 22:32 KJV)*

Months later, he called; his voice alive with joy. "Pastor, I've returned to serving in my church. I serve with the prayer ministry team. I can't describe how alive I feel!"

I rejoiced with him encouraging him to embrace his new journey. Once again, I had witnessed what happens when a heart returns to the altar—restoration always follows.

The altar isn't just a place; it's an encounter. It's where lost sons and daughters hear the Father's voice again. It's where ashes become beauty and silence turns into song.

YOUR HEART, THE ALTAR WHERE TRUE PRAYER BEGINS

There's a sacred place within every believer—a place not made of stone or wood, but of spirit and surrender. It's the heart serving as an altar. It's where heaven leans close and where your truest prayers are born.

The heart is where the real work of prayer begins. It's not in the beauty of your words or the length of your devotion, but in the honesty of your stance before God. You can say all the right things and still not touch heaven. But when your heart bows low, when pride melts into surrender, and love becomes your language—God draws near.

Jesus said, "God is Spirit, and those who worship Him must worship in spirit and truth." (John 4:24 NKJV) The heart is the only altar fit for such worship, because it is where spirit and truth meet.

When you pray from the heart, heaven recognizes the sound—it's the sound of authenticity. It's what David meant when he said, "You desire truth in the inward parts." (Psalm 51:6 NKJV)

This is where prayer ceases to be performance and becomes presence. It's where you stop trying to impress God and start inviting Him.

Throughout Scripture, God commanded His people to build altars. From Noah to Abraham, from Elijah to Israel's priests, every altar had one purpose—to host His presence.

But now, under grace, God has chosen a new altar—your heart.

The Old Testament altars were temporary. They required stones, fire, and sacrifice. But at Calvary, Jesus made the ultimate offering, and the fire of His Spirit now burns within us. The altar has moved from a mountain to a man, from ritual to relationship, from a temple made with hands to a heart yielded in prayer.

It's no longer about location—it's about condition.

Leviticus 6:13 declared, "A fire shall always be burning on the altar; it shall never go out." That same fire is meant to burn in your heart. It's the fire of devotion, the flame of fellowship, the warmth of intimacy.

But like the priests of old, we must tend it. Prayer is how we keep the fire alive.

If you neglect prayer, the flame grows dim. If you guard it, the altar glows with presence.

Every time you pray sincerely, you're laying wood on the fire again—repentance, thanksgiving, worship, surrender. The altar of your heart becomes a living furnace of communion with God.

THE FIRE THAT REFINES

Every altar requires a sacrifice, and every sacrifice requires fire. In prayer, that fire is not destructive—it's purifying. When you come before God, you bring not only your faith but also your flesh—your motives, your fears, your hidden struggles. And on that altar, the Spirit begins His refining work.

The altar exposes what performance hides. It brings the unseen into the open. It burns away the pride that disguises itself as strength and the bitterness that disguises itself as righteousness.

Malachi 3:3 describes God as a refiner and purifier of silver. The refiner's fire is not to destroy but to cleanse until the reflection of the Creator shines through the metal. That's what the Spirit does in prayer.

He burns away what's false until only truth remains. He consumes what is temporary to reveal what is eternal.

It's not always comfortable. There are prayers that bring tears, prayers that expose wounds, prayers that challenge your obedience. But if you stay on the altar, you'll emerge renewed, transformed, radiant with glory.

SURRENDER: THE SACRIFICE GOD CANNOT RESIST

The altar of prayer is where surrender becomes sacred. Romans 12:1 says, "Present your bodies a living sacrifice, holy, acceptable to God, which is your reasonable service. "God doesn't want lifeless offerings—He wants living ones. He doesn't require the blood of bulls or goats—He desires the beating heart of His children.

When you pray with a surrendered heart, you're saying, "Lord, I'm not just giving You my request; I'm giving You myself."

True prayer begins when you stop using words to move God and start allowing His presence to move you. That's when you begin to sense the exchange happening—the weight lifting, the peace descending, the Spirit interceding.

The altar is not a place you visit—it's a place you become.

THE BROKEN HEART GOD LOVES

If you've ever prayed through tears, you've already been at the altar. David wrote, "The sacrifices of God are a broken spirit, a broken and a contrite heart—these, O God, You will not despise." (Psalm 51:17 NKJV)

A broken heart isn't a disqualified heart—it's a ready one. When pride cracks and self-sufficiency crumbles, God moves in with mercy. The enemy will tell you that your pain disqualifies you. But in truth, your pain is often what positions you. The pieces of your heart become the offering that heaven accepts.

I've seen this countless times in ministry. People come to the altar ashamed of their weakness, convinced they've failed God. But as they kneel, the fire of grace touches them—and what was broken becomes beautiful again. The same place that hurt becomes the place God heals.

WHEN THE ALTAR IS NEGLECTED

If prayer keeps the altar burning, neglect lets the flame grow cold. When your heart drifts from communion, you can still look spiritual outwardly, but something sacred fades inwardly. You start going through the motions—reading without revelation, worshiping without wonder, praying without passion. That's the smoke without the fire.

The Spirit begins to whisper, "Come back." Not in condemnation, but in invitation. He doesn't need your performance; He desires your presence. He wants to rebuild the altar of intimacy within you.

1 Kings 18 tells how Elijah rebuilt the broken altar before calling down fire from heaven. That's where many believers are today—the altar has been neglected, the stones scattered by distraction, but God is calling us to rebuild.

And when you do, fire falls again. Presence returns. Passion rekindles.

THE ALTAR IS WHERE HEAVEN MEETS EARTH

Every genuine move of God begins at an altar. That's where conviction is born, where decisions are made, where destinies shift. But not all altars are built of wood and stone. Some are built in bedrooms, in quiet cars, in late-night prayers whispered through tears.

Wherever the heart bows, heaven responds.

Your altar might not look like much to others, but to God it's sacred ground. Because the altar of your heart is where His fire rests.

In those moments when you're alone with Him—no audience, no spotlight, no applause—you become a living temple filled with His glory.

That's where the fragrance of your prayer rises like incense before Him. Revelation 5:8 paints it so vividly: "The prayers of the saints" are like golden bowls of incense filling the heavens.

Every time you pray, every time you worship, every time you surrender—your altar fills heaven with fragrance.

THE ALTAR AND THE ANOINTING

If you want greater anointing, spend more time at the altar with the One who anoints. Every spiritual mantle is born out of intimacy. Every sermon that carries power was first birthed in secret prayer. Every worship that carries presence flows from an altar that burns within.

Anointing is never random—it's a residue from time spent in His presence.

Moses' face shone after he spoke with God. Elijah's fire fell after he rebuilt the altar. Jesus' ministry began after prayer in the wilderness.

Before God uses you publicly, He refines you privately. The altar is where He shapes your heart for His glory.

And if you want to carry His presence beyond moments—into meetings, homes, cities—you must live as one whose altar never goes out.

THE ALTAR AND INTIMACY

The altar is not only a place of refining—it's a place of communion. It's where you feel His whisper in your spirit and sense His peace wrapping around your thoughts. It's where tears become language, silence becomes worship, and stillness becomes strength.

There are things God will only say to you at the altar—truths too sacred for the noise of the crowd.

That's why intimacy cannot be rushed. You must linger long enough for His presence to settle, for your soul to quiet, for His voice to rise above your emotions.

The altar of your heart is where relationships deepen. It's where prayer stops being something you do and becomes who you are.

When your heart is the altar, every moment can be prayer—a walk, a drive, a breath, a whisper. You live in communion, not just communication.

GUARDING THE ALTAR OF YOUR HEART

If your heart is the altar, then guarding it is your sacred duty. Proverbs 4:23 says, "Keep your heart with all diligence, for out of it spring the issues of life."

What you allow into your heart fuels or extinguishes your fire. Bitterness is water on the flame. Gratitude is the oil that makes it burn brighter.

Guard your heart against offense, distraction, and unbelief. They are thieves of devotion. Feed it with the Word, worship, and quiet reflection.

The altar of your heart must remain pure—not perfect, but surrendered. Because purity attracts presence, and presence changes everything.

Reflection

What does your personal altar look like right now—burning bright or in need of rebuilding?

Are there areas of your heart that need to be placed on the altar—fear, pride, bitterness, control?

How can you cultivate daily intimacy at the altar of your heart this week?

Prayer

Father, thank You for making my heart Your dwelling place. Teach me to tend the fire of prayer and keep my altar pure. I bring You my whole heart—every wound, every weakness, every desire.

Refine me in Your presence until all that remains is love and surrender. Let my heart burn with devotion and overflow with worship. When I grow distracted, draw me back to the altar again. When I feel distant, remind me that You never left.

Let the fire on my heart's altar never go out. In Jesus' name, Amen.

The Fire That Never Dies

The altar is not a moment—it's a lifestyle. It's the continual offering of your heart, morning by morning, moment by moment. And the promise still stands: "The fire shall always be burning on the altar; it shall never go out."

Once you've encountered the fire of His presence, you'll never settle for ashes again.

Something holy happens when the heart stays surrendered — Heaven finds a home.

Prayer on the Next Level

When your heart truly becomes the altar where prayer begins, something shifts. You stop trying to reach God through effort and begin flowing with Him through intimacy. The altar becomes alive—not with words you've memorized, but with the fire of communion that only the Holy Spirit can sustain.

There comes a point in prayer when your heart longs to say more than words can carry. Your spirit begins to reach for expression beyond what your mind can form. It's in those sacred moments that the Holy Spirit steps in—not to replace your voice, but to fill it. He gives you a language that heaven understands—a language not learned, but imparted.

Praying in tongues isn't about emotional display; it's about spiritual alignment. It's heaven breathing through your humanity. It's your spirit partnering with His, releasing mysteries, intercession, and praise that words could never capture.

At that altar, prayer becomes more than conversation—it becomes communion. And in that communion, the Spirit begins to speak through you.

In the next chapter, we'll enter that holy mystery—The Language of the Spirit: Praying in Tongues—and discover how God gives your spirit a voice that carries the sound of heaven itself.

CHAPTER 8

THE LANGUAGE OF THE SPIRIT: PRAYING IN THE SPIRIT

There's a kind of prayer that can't be explained — it can only be experienced. It rises beyond emotion, vocabulary, and intellect. It doesn't come from the head but from the heart — from that sacred space within where the Holy Spirit Himself begins to pray through you.

In those moments, it's no longer you searching for words; it's heaven giving your heart a voice. The language may sound unfamiliar to your ears, but to the Father, it's music — pure, unfiltered worship born of surrender and love.

That's what it means to pray in the Spirit. It's when heaven borrows your voice to speak mysteries your mind cannot grasp, yet your spirit knows are true.

Paul wrote, *"The Spirit also helps in our weaknesses. For we do not know what we should pray for as we ought, but the Spirit Himself makes intercession for us with groanings which cannot be uttered."* (Romans 8:26–27 NKJV)

Praying in the Spirit is not an emotional release — it's divine partnership. It's heaven and earth praying together through a yielded vessel. It's you and God breathing the same prayer from two sides of eternity.

HE THAT SPEAKS IN TONGUES SPEAKS TO GOD, NOT TO MEN

Paul declared, *"For he who speaks in a tongue does not speak to men but to God, for no one understands him; however, in the Spirit he speaks mysteries."* (1 Corinthians 14:2 NKJV)

When you speak in tongues, you are not addressing people — you are conversing directly with the Father. Every syllable is sacred. Every sound carries divine intention. You are speaking from your spirit, not your mind.

Tongues are not emotional overflow — they are spiritual encryption. They are heaven's secret language, wrapped in mystery and sealed by the Spirit. When you pray in tongues, the enemy can't intercept your words, and doubt can't distort them. You are communicating with the throne of God in a code that only heaven understands.

It's divine encryption — a prayer language that can't be hacked by the enemy, manipulated by fear, or polluted by self-interest. Your mind may not understand it, but your spirit does. God hears it perfectly.

This is the beauty of praying in tongues: it's the purest form of communion. The words you speak bypass the limits of intellect and flow directly into the heart of God. It's your spirit speaking to His — an exchange so holy that heaven moves at the sound of it.

When you pray in the Spirit, you are not trying to convince God to act; you are partnering with what He already desires to do. It's not persuasion — it's participation. Heaven flows through you.

WHEN WORDS RUN OUT

There comes a moment when human language fails — when you've cried every tear, prayed every verse, and spoken every plea you know. You reach the end of yourself, and yet, your heart still longs to say more.

That's where the Holy Spirit steps in.

He doesn't silence you — He joins you. He gives voice to what you can't articulate. He takes your weakness and turns it into worship.

Sometimes those prayers come out as whispers, sometimes as weeping, sometimes as syllables you don't understand — but heaven recognizes every one of them. Those moments are not empty noise; they are sacred exchanges between your spirit and the Spirit of God.

You may not understand what you're saying, but the Father does — and in His presence, even your groans carry weight.

THE LIMITS OF THE MIND

Your mind is a gift, but it can't take the lead in prayer. It analyzes, reasons, and plans — but prayer isn't a mental exercise. It's communion.

Paul said, *"For if I pray in a tongue, my spirit prays, but my understanding is unfruitful."* (1 Corinthians 14:14 NKJV)

That means prayer in the Spirit doesn't flow from knowledge — it flows from relationship. Your mind might not comprehend it, but your spirit rejoices in it.

The Holy Spirit prays from a higher place. He prays from perfect perspective — from the vantage point of heaven. He sees what's ahead, what's hidden, what's possible, and what's necessary. When you let Him lead, your prayers align perfectly with the will of God, even when you don't fully understand what's happening.

Your mind prays from what it knows; the Spirit prays from what He sees. And because He searches the deep things of God (1 Corinthians 2:10), your prayer begins to harmonize with heaven's heartbeat.

PARTNERSHIP, NOT PERFORMANCE

Praying in the Spirit isn't about losing control — it's about surrendering it. It's not strange or forced; it's the natural expression of a heart that trusts the Holy Spirit more than its own understanding.

When you yield your voice to the Spirit, you are saying, "Lord, I trust You with my tongue, my thoughts, and my direction." That's humility — and humility always invites power.

As you pray, you may sense the Spirit leading you to intercede for someone, to declare breakthrough, or to worship with fresh passion. Follow those promptings. They are not random thoughts — they are divine instructions. Heaven is moving through your willingness.

This is what partnership looks like — heaven using your voice to release God's will on earth. Prayer becomes less about what you're saying and more about who's speaking through you.

WHEN PRAYER BECOMES POWER

When the Spirit prays through you, something changes. Fear loses its grip. Peace begins to rise. Confusion gives way to clarity. You're no longer begging for victory — you're praying from it.

This is the authority Jesus spoke of when He said, *"Whatever you bind on earth will be bound in heaven, and whatever you loose on earth will be loosed in heaven."* (Matthew 18:18 NKJV)

That's not arrogance — that's agreement. You're not commanding God; you're aligning with Him. You become an instrument of His power, declaring what heaven has already decreed.

When you pray in the Spirit, your words are not empty sounds — they are declarations of divine intent. Heaven moves when faith speaks, and praying in tongues is faith in its purest sound.

HOW TO RECEIVE THE HOLY SPIRIT

The baptism of the Holy Spirit isn't reserved for a select few — it's the Father's promise for every believer.

Jesus said, *"If you then, being evil, know how to give good gifts to your children, how much more will your heavenly Father give the Holy Spirit to those who ask Him!"* (Luke 11:13 NKJV)

Receiving the Holy Spirit begins with hunger. You don't earn Him; you simply open your heart and receive.

In Acts 2, the disciples didn't strive — they waited. And when the wind of heaven came, everything changed. The same Spirit who filled that upper room still fills hungry hearts today.

Here's how to receive:

Believe the Holy Spirit is God's gift to you through Jesus Christ.

Ask in faith, trusting the Father's goodness.

Surrender your will, your voice, and your control.

Expect to receive — because He always fills the hearts that are ready.

You might feel warmth, joy, or an overwhelming peace. You might sense a language forming within you — don't resist it. Yield to it. The Spirit won't force His way in; He flows where He's invited.

Speaking in tongues isn't the goal — it's the overflow. The true miracle is His indwelling presence.

PRAYER TO RECEIVE THE HOLY SPIRIT

Father, I come in the name of Jesus, Your Son and my Savior.

You promised to pour out Your Spirit on all flesh, and today, I open my heart to receive.

Holy Spirit, come. Fill me now. Saturate every part of my being with Your presence.

Cleanse my heart, renew my mind, and speak through my lips.

I surrender my thoughts, my will, and my control.

I receive the baptism of the Holy Spirit by faith right now.

Let rivers of living water flow from within me.

Let Your heavenly language rise from my spirit.

Empower me to pray, to love, to serve, and to walk in Your truth.

Thank You, Father, for filling me with Your Spirit.

In Jesus' mighty name, Amen.

STAYING SENSITIVE TO THE SPIRIT

Praying in the Spirit isn't a one-time experience; it's a lifestyle. The more you yield to His presence, the more natural His voice becomes.

He will nudge you — in worship, in stillness, sometimes even in the middle of a busy day. When you sense His prompting, don't ignore it. Heaven's invitations often come as gentle whispers.

The Spirit's voice is soft but certain. It carries peace, not pressure. When He speaks, respond quickly. When He stirs your heart, linger. When He leads, follow. Miracles often begin in the moments we almost overlook.

Stay sensitive. Stay surrendered. Stay in tune with the Spirit who never stops interceding through you.

REFLECTION QUESTIONS

Have you received the baptism of the Holy Spirit, or are you still longing for it?

What fears or misconceptions have kept you from fully yielding to His presence?

How might your prayer life deepen if you prayed more in the Spirit than in your own strength?

Prayer

Holy Spirit, thank You for being my Helper in prayer.

When my words run dry, You give me language.

When my strength fades, You give me power.

Teach me to yield completely — to stop leading and start listening.

Fill me afresh every day.

Let my prayers carry heaven's weight, not my worry.

Pray through me until earth echoes with heaven's voice.

In Jesus' name, Amen.

The Power of Partnering with the Spirit

Praying in the Spirit teaches you how to yield — to let heaven shape your words and carry your prayers where human understanding cannot go. But once you've learned to yield, something deeper happens:

The Spirit doesn't just speak *through* you — He begins to speak *as* you.

Your prayers carry the authority of heaven because they originate from the heart of God. The same Spirit who intercedes now empowers you to declare, decree, and walk in victory.

That's the next dimension of prayer — when Spirit-filled prayer becomes Spirit-led dominion.

And that's where we're headed next — into *Intercessory Prayer,* where the Spirit not only moves in you but through you to shift the world around you.

CHAPTER 9

INTERCESSORY PRAYER: PRAYER THAT MOVES HEAVEN AND CHANGES EARTH

PRAYER THAT MOVES HEAVEN AND CHANGES EARTH

Some prayers are born out of need—but others are born out of burden. Intercession belongs to the latter. It's the kind of prayer that doesn't ask for blessings; it stands in the gap between Heaven's mercy and Earth's pain.

When you become an intercessor, you begin to feel what God feels. You sense the weight of others' pain and the pull of His compassion at the same time. It's not a role you choose—it's a calling that chooses you.

There have been times I've gone to pray for my own needs, but before I could finish, the Spirit shifted my focus to someone else. Their faces would flash before my mind, or their names would surface in my spirit, and I'd feel a divine urgency—an assignment from Heaven. That's intercession. It's when your heart becomes a bridge God can walk across to reach another.

THE HEART OF AN INTERCESSOR

Intercession begins with love. Before you can pray effectively for others, your heart must break for what breaks God's. That's why the Holy Spirit often calls intercessors out of their comfort zones—because you can't stand in the gap if you're unwilling to feel the gap.

Abraham felt it when he stood before God on behalf of Sodom (Genesis 18). His prayer wasn't casual; it was bold, persistent, almost pleading. "Will You also destroy the righteous with the wicked?" he asked. Abraham wasn't trying to manipulate God—he was mirroring His mercy.

That's the essence of intercession. You begin to echo the heartbeat of Heaven. You start praying not just for outcomes, but for souls.

When your heart aligns with God's compassion, your words carry authority. Love is what gives prayer its power. The prayers that move Heaven are the ones birthed in compassion, not in pride.

STANDING IN THE GAP

Ezekiel 22:30 says,

"I sought for a man among them who would make a wall and stand in the gap before Me on behalf of the land, that I should not destroy it; but I found no one."

That verse still impacts me every time I read it. God was looking for a partner—someone who would intercede, someone who would care enough to pray.

He wasn't searching for perfection; He was searching for participation. Intercessors are not super-spiritual people—they're simply *available* people. God doesn't need your perfection to move; He needs your permission.

When you say, "Lord, use me," Heaven takes you at your word. The Holy Spirit begins to awaken a sensitivity inside you. You'll start feeling spiritual burdens before situations even unfold. Sometimes you'll find yourself praying for people you've never met or nations you've never seen. That's not a coincidence—it's cooperation with the Spirit of God.

THE WEIGHT AND WONDER OF BURDEN

I remember that night in the early 80s—long before seatbelt laws, when my father drove his 1968 Chevy Caprice, a solid car but no match for a head-on collision.

At exactly 2:00 a.m., the Holy Spirit woke me with an urgent, overwhelming burden to pray. I didn't know why. I didn't know who it was for. All I knew was that Heaven was pressing on my spirit, and I had to answer.

So I got out of bed, knelt down, and began to pray in the Spirit. For an hour I interceded—waves of urgency rising and falling—until suddenly the burden lifted, and a deep, quiet peace settled over me. I had no idea what was happening at that very moment.

About an hour after I went back to sleep, the phone rang. My father had been in a head-on collision. His car was completely totaled.

Later, he told me what happened inside those terrifying seconds. He said he saw the other car suddenly swerve into his lane—a drunk driver. All he had time to cry out was, "Lord, help me!"

When the impact hit, his body lunged forward—he should have gone straight through the windshield. But instead, he felt a strong hand press against his chest and gently lay him across the bench seat. Metal twisted, glass exploded through the air... but inside, he felt calm—supernaturally calm.

He told me, "I can't explain it, but in the middle of everything, I felt somebody praying for me."

And I was. Fifteen minutes before the accident at 2:15 a.m., and for the forty-five harrowing minutes they struggled to pull him from the wreck and rush him to the hospital, I was on my knees, interceding—though I didn't yet understand why.

When first responders examined him, they were stunned—no broken bones, no internal injuries, no head trauma. They had seen people die in cars with far less damage.

When my father and I compared the timing—the moment the Holy Spirit woke me, the moment he cried out to God, the moment of the crash—we both knew unmistakably: God had intervened. Prayer had built a shield around him. Heaven had reached down and preserved his life.

Intercession may interrupt your sleep, your schedule, your comfort—but it will never be wasted. You may not always know what your obedience prevents or what miracle it releases... but Heaven knows.

And sometimes, God lets you hear the miracle from the one who survived it.

JESUS, THE MODEL INTERCESSOR
The greatest intercessor of all is Jesus Himself. Hebrews 7:25 says,

"He ever lives to make intercession for us."

Think about that. The Son of God—resurrected, glorified, enthroned—still prays. Even now, His ministry continues through intercession.

When you intercede, you are joining Him in that ongoing heavenly assignment. You're not just praying *to* God; you're praying *with* Him.

The Spirit in you, joins the Son before the Father in perfect unity.

That's why the devil fights intercession so fiercely—it's the closest you can come to standing in Christ's shoes. It's the place where your compassion becomes a conduit for His power.

THE COST OF COMPASSION

Intercession is beautiful, but it's not without cost. To carry others in prayer, you must let go of indifference. To stand in the gap, you must be willing to feel the gap.

Moses felt it when Israel sinned against God. He fell on his face and cried,

"Oh, this people has sinned a great sin... yet now, if You will forgive their sin—but if not, blot me, I pray You, out of Your book." (Exodus 32:31–32).

Moses' love was costly. He identified so deeply with the people that he was willing to risk everything for their redemption. That's the kind of compassion intercession produces—it makes you love beyond convenience.

WHEN PRAYER BECOMES PARTNERSHIP

At its core, intercession is partnership. It's not about convincing God to act; it's about agreeing with His heart until Heaven and Earth align.

When you intercede, you become a vessel through which His mercy flows. You become a channel of grace on the earth.

Romans 8:27 says,

"The Spirit intercedes for the saints according to the will of God."

That means every time you pray under the Spirit's influence, you're praying God's perfect will—even when you don't know what it is.

There are prayers you pray with understanding, and then there are groanings of the Spirit—deeper than language, stronger than logic. Those are the prayers that shake nations and rescue souls.

THANKSGIVING AS A PART OF INTERCESSORY PRAYER

I heard about a woman at a friend of mine's church who received an intercessory assignment that transformed her entire family. Her husband had walked away from God, and every attempt to reach him seemed futile.

But one night during prayer, she felt the Spirit whisper,

"Stop pleading—start partnering."

From that moment on, her prayers changed. Instead of begging God to fix him, she began to thank God for drawing him. She started interceding in tongues daily, not from despair but from authority.

Months later, her husband walked into church, tears streaming down his face, saying, "I don't know what happened, but something's been pulling me back."

That's intercession—it doesn't just ask for change; it births it.

THE POWER OF INTERCESSORY PRAYER AND FAITH

Faith is often tested at the very threshold of breakthrough. What looks like a closed door may, in truth, be a test of whether you will pray from fear or stand in faith.

Over a couple of decades ago, we were in the process of acquiring the very building our church occupies today. The owner had assured me it was ours—he only needed a few papers to clear on his end. Confident of that promise, and the peace of God I received before proceeding; we planned our grand opening and began remodeling.

The key had already been given, and work was in motion. The hum of hammers and saws filled the air, and I felt the momentum of a dream finally coming together.

Then came the call.

The realtor's voice carried a weight that didn't belong to good news. "Dr. Simpson, there's been a development," he said. My heart sank. I thought perhaps another delay—but this was different.

We met at the property. His steps were heavy, his face torn between duty and dread. Inside, the workers were busy—walls going up, floors being laid. He saw it all and turned pale. The noise drowned his words, so we stepped outside.

He drew a long breath and said, "Dr. Simpson, I'm afraid I have bad news. The deal's in jeopardy. Other 'interests' have stepped in. The owner may back out completely."

I felt that old, familiar pain. The memory of the first building we'd lost—the deceit, the disappointment—rushed back like a shadow from the past. Here I was again, standing in a parking lot, staring at what felt like another broken promise.

He looked at me with pity. "You've already invested thousands, and I doubt you'll recover much. Stop now before you lose any more."

Something rose up on the inside of me. A holy boldness. The kind that does not come from personality—it comes from Presence.

"We're not going to lose this building." I said firmly, meeting his eyes. No yelling. No anger. Just words spoken with quiet conviction."

The moment those words left my mouth, fear broke off me. Faith rose up and took its place. The atmosphere shifted—not outwardly, but within. I wasn't denying the facts; I was declaring the truth.

Later that evening, I told my wife what had happened. Without hesitation, she said, "The devil is a liar! He's not taking that property from us." She searched my face, concerned about how I was dealing with this for the second time. She saw nothing but faith and determination.

Then she embraced me and said, "Baby, you know God is for us, and as you say after every sermon, "If God is for you, it really doesn't matter who is against you, for you have already won! And we said, "Amen to that!

We prayed together and thanked God for the victory before seeing any evidence of it.

But that night, while the house was still, fear tried to find its way back. I woke with the weight of dread pressing on my chest. Every fearful thought imaginable whispered in the dark: What if it falls through again? What if this time, you've gone too far?

So I rose from bed and began to pray—quietly but fervently. I rebuked fear. I worshiped until peace returned. Then I felt the Holy Spirit prompting me: Walk the property.

As I got dressed, my wife stirred. "Where are you going?"

"I'm going to walk around the property and declare God's promises," I said softly.

Without hesitation, she got out of bed and started getting dressed. "I'm coming too."

I tried to reason with her—it was two in the morning, dark, unsafe—but she simply said, "If it's too dangerous for me, then it's too dangerous for you. The same God who'll protect you will protect me."

And that settled it.

We drove through the quiet streets; the moonlight glinting off the windshield. As we neared the church property, my wife and I began speaking faith-filled confessions. After arriving, we walked the entire three and a half acres—hand in hand, declaring the Word of the Lord. We claimed the land for the Kingdom. We decreed that no weapon formed against us would prosper, that every adversary would stumble and fall.

We prayed and declared until the night itself seemed to listen.

The next day, the general contractor came to me with the next phase of remodeling and a new invoice. Fifty thousand dollars more. Logic said to pause, but faith said to proceed. I gave the order to proceed.

That wasn't recklessness; it was obedience. Faith acts on what it hears from God, not what it sees in the natural.

The following day, my realtor arrived with a look of astonishment written all over his face. "Dr. Simpson," he said, shaking his head, "you must truly be a man of faith. The owner called me this morning and said, *'I can't do that preacher like that. Not giving him the property has really been bothering me.'* He's decided to honor the deal. Not only that, he gave us additional property located near that of the building. Praise God!

And just like that—what seemed lost was restored. The property was ours. **Debt-free. It was a "suddenly miracle!"**

We shouted, praised and worshiped. The land we had walked in the dark was now illuminated by the light of victory.

It's remarkable that a businessman—a man driven by profit—still had a conscience, something the deceitful pastor and his board clearly lacked. What they intended for evil, God repurposed for our good. Listen, I declare today that the same redemptive power is at work in your situation. God wants to take what was meant to harm you and transform it into the very thing that will bless, strengthen, and elevate you.

THE CALL TO STAND IN THE GAP

God is still looking for intercessors today. You don't need a platform—you need a prayer room. You don't need eloquence—you need empathy. You don't need recognition—you need obedience.

When you make yourself available, Heaven will assign you burdens. Some will be light and brief; others will be heavy and ongoing. But every one of them carries eternal impact.

There's no higher calling than to be trusted by God with His heart for others.

HOW TO CULTIVATE AN INTERCESSOR'S HEART

Pray for sensitivity. Ask the Holy Spirit to awaken compassion within you.

Respond quickly. When you feel a burden, pray immediately. Don't delay Heaven's assignment.

Pray in the Spirit. The most powerful intercession happens when your spirit joins His.

Keep confidentiality. What God reveals in prayer is sacred. Guard it with integrity.

Rejoice when peace comes. When the burden lifts, give thanks—He's already moved.

Reflection

Has God ever placed someone or something heavy on your heart to pray for? How did you respond?

What keeps you from fully embracing the role of an intercessor?

How can you cultivate a greater sensitivity to the Holy Spirit's prompting in prayer?

Prayer

Father,

Thank You for trusting me with Your heart. Teach me to stand in the gap with compassion and boldness. Let Your Spirit pray through me when words fall short. Break my heart for what breaks Yours, and fill me with faith to believe that prayer can change anything—because it connects to the God who can do everything. Use me, Lord, as an instrument of Your mercy.

In Jesus' name, Amen.

Intercession teaches you the compassion of prayer.

Agreement reveals the **government** of prayer.

One teaches you to carry the burdens of others.

The other teaches you to **join faith with others** to enforce Heaven's will.

And that's where the next revelation begins —

in the space where Heaven is ready...

but Heaven will not move until earth stands together.

When Heaven Waits for Earth: The Power of Agreement in Prayer

CHAPTER 10

WHEN HEAVEN WAITS FOR EARTH: THE POWER OF AGREEMENT IN PRAYER

Prayer is not a performance; it is a partnership. Heaven is not moved by the most eloquent voice but by the most united hearts. When two believers truly agree—spirit to spirit, will to will—something shifts in the unseen. The heavens lean close. Power begins to flow.

"Again I say to you that if two of you agree on earth concerning anything that they ask,
it will be done for them by My Father in heaven."
— Matthew 18:19, NKJV

Agreement is more than repeating the same words. It is two lives yielding to the same Lord, two hearts resting under the same authority, two minds saying, "Your will be done." Harmony is the language of heaven. The Father, Son, and Holy Spirit never move in discord, and they invite us to pray from that same unity.

HEAVEN RESPONDS TO HARMONY

From the beginning, God revealed that power flows through partnership. *"It is not good that man should be alone."* (Genesis 2:18) That word is bigger than companionship; it is a call to collaboration. Creation was shaped by a God who said, "Let Us," and His Kingdom advances when His people say, "Let us" with Him.

When you agree with another believer, faith multiplies. You move from solitary strength to shared authority. Jesus did not say, "If a thousand agree." He said, *"If two of you agree..."* Two hearts aligned with the Father can move what one heart can only nudge. The enemy knows this. That is why he fights unity harder than he fights prayer. A divided church cannot shake a united hell. But when humility replaces pride, when forgiveness silences offense, and when love takes the lead—heaven answers without hesitation.

THE SOUND OF ONE ACCORD

Agreement begins before a single word is spoken. It begins where hearts bow. You can pray the same sentence and still be out of step if your spirits are not one. But when unity is genuine, faith takes on a symphonic quality.

After Peter and John were threatened, they returned to the believers and lifted their voices together. Scripture records, *"When they had prayed, the place where they were assembled together was shaken; and they were all filled with the Holy Spirit."* (Acts 4:31, NKJV) The shaking was not judgment; it was heaven's affirmation. God moved because His people moved as one.

Harmony formed a highway for His glory.

WHEN HEAVEN WAITS FOR EARTH

There are moments when heaven stands ready but waits for earth to agree. God said through Ezekiel, *"I sought for a man… who would stand in the gap before Me on behalf of the land."* (Ezekiel 22:30) The will of God desired to break in, but the voice of agreement was missing.

Prayer is not about persuading God; it is about partnering with Him. The will of God must be echoed by the faith of man. When you align your heart with His and join hands with another believer, you release permission for heaven to intervene. Agreement opens the gate.

Faith in Harmony

A woman in our church had battled a long illness and had grown weary. "Do you still believe?" I asked. Tears gathered. "I do… but I'm tired."

"Then let's agree," I said. "I'll hold faith where you feel empty, and we'll stand until the report changes."

We didn't shout. We didn't strive. We simply agreed. The atmosphere softened. Peace took the room. Days later, the doctor's note read, "Condition improving rapidly." Agreement amplified what personal prayer had been pressing against. Heaven met us in the space between clasped hands and surrendered hearts.

The Power of Corporate Unity

Some miracles require more than private devotion; they require corporate agreement. *"They were all with one accord in one place."* (Acts 2) Then came the *suddenly*. The sequence matters—one accord precedes suddenly. Unity is the womb of visitation.

The early church did not gather for show; they gathered for surrender.

Every "amen" was alignment. Every lifted hand, a declaration of oneness. The enemy does not fear large crowds; he fears united ones. Even at Babel, God observed, *"Now nothing that they propose to do will be withheld from them."* (Genesis 11:6, NKJV) If rebel unity holds such force, how much more when the righteous unite under the Spirit of Truth?

The Flow of the Anointing

"Behold, how good and how pleasant it is for brethren to dwell together in unity! It is like the precious oil upon the head... running down..." (Psalm 133) Oil represents the anointing—the felt evidence of God's presence. Oil does not fall where there is friction; it flows where there is fellowship. The anointing that rests on the Head—Christ—moves freely through His Body when we dwell together in unity.

Disagreement dries up the flow. Harmony keeps it fresh. Jesus sent His disciples two by two because partnership multiplies authority. *One can chase a thousand, and two can put ten thousand to flight.* (Deuteronomy 32:30) Each time two believers agree in Jesus' name, heaven draws near to listen.

When Agreement Costs You

Agreement often asks for humility. You cannot hold offense and hold hands in prayer at the same time. Jesus said, *"If you bring your gift to the altar, and there remember that your brother has something against you... first be reconciled."* (Matthew 5:23–24) God values reconciliation more than ritual because broken relationships break spiritual rhythm. Forgiveness restores the cadence of the Spirit. To agree with heaven, release what binds you on earth.

When Heaven Finds Its Sound

"Where two or three are gathered together in My name, I am there in the midst of them." (Matthew 18:20) Gathered in His name means gathered under His lordship—His character, His authority, His way. That is

why miracles often rise in atmospheres of unity: Jesus inhabits the space between agreeing hearts. Heaven is not waiting for eloquence; heaven is waiting for alignment.

Reflection Questions

Who is God inviting you to join with in prayer so that faith can multiply?

What offense or misunderstanding must be released so unity can be restored?

Which situation in your life requires moving from private petition to shared agreement?

Prayer

Father, thank You for the gift of agreement. Bring my heart into harmony with Yours and with those You've joined to me in Christ. Uproot pride and offense. Heal places where love has grown thin. Teach me to pray in one accord, so that Your will is done on earth as it is in heaven. Let unity release the oil of Your anointing and let our "amen" become a sound You cannot ignore. In Jesus' name, Amen.

The Sound That Shakes the Earth

When believers agree, heaven does not merely hear—it responds. Every "amen" becomes a tremor in the unseen. Chains loosen. Walls give way. Faith ignites. And yet, agreement is not the destination; it is the doorway. When hearts become one, God draws us to the true altar—not a stage, not a platform, but the inner place where prayer lives and breathes.

"Intercession gives birth to compassion. The power of agreement multiplies effectiveness. But authority—spiritual authority—establishes command. In the next chapter, we'll uncover how to pray from your position in Christ—*seated with Him in heavenly places,* carrying divine authority that hell cannot ignore. Get ready for the revelation of **"Praying With Authority."**

CHAPTER 11

WHEN FAITH IS TESTED: PRAYER BECOMES A LIFELINE

TRUSTING GOD THROUGH BROKEN PROMISES

Every believer faces a defining moment when the beauty of worship meets the heavy pressures of life. The song that once flowed with joy becomes the quiet cry you whisper through tears. It's that sacred place where pain tests your reverence, and faith must rise above feelings and become endurance.

Adoration teaches you to lift your eyes in awe, but prayer teaches you to hold on when the storm rages. What's birthed in the stillness of His presence must be sustained in the pressure of His purpose. And it's there—in the tension between what you hoped for and what now hurts—that prayer becomes real.

There are seasons when prayer stops being a comfort and becomes a necessity. It's no longer something you say—it becomes something you breathe. Every whisper becomes a reach for God's hand when you can no longer stand on your own. Prayer becomes the thread that holds your soul together—the lifeline that keeps your spirit from sinking.

I've walked through many seasons in ministry—some overflowing with joy, others marked by deep disappointment—but one in particular tested my faith in ways I could never have imagined. It began with a handshake that sealed a promise and ended with heartbreak that shattered everything I thought I understood about trust.

In that season, I learned a truth that only trials can teach: **faith is not proven in victory—it's proven in vulnerability.** It isn't tested when everything works out, but when nothing makes sense and you still choose to believe.

And it's in moments like these that your theology meets your reality. You discover what you truly believe about God's goodness, His faithfulness, and His timing. Not the version you preach or quote—but the one your heart clings to when all else falls away.

VEILS OF DECEPTION

We were in the process of purchasing a church building near the heart of the city—a miracle in the making. For years, we had prayed for such an opportunity: a larger space to grow, to reach more souls, and to expand the work of the ministry. The location was perfect. The facility was ideal. Everything appeared divinely orchestrated.

But behind the scenes, deception was already at work. The pastor and board of that church were not negotiating in good faith. Unbeknownst to us, they were using our offer as leverage against another church—a silent competition we didn't even know existed.

After much prayer, faith-filled preparation, and a substantial down payment, we secured a loan from a local bank. I remember walking into the church office—my wife beside me, our leaders with us—as we presented the Letter of Intent for a loan exceeding half a million dollars, the full purchase price.

It felt like destiny—the culmination of years of intercession, fasting, and faith.

Yet as I handed the letter to the pastor, something in my spirit stirred—a subtle uneasiness I couldn't quite name. I brushed it aside, reassuring myself, "We've prayed. Surely this is the fulfillment of God's promise."

But I would soon learn a hard truth: discernment ignored becomes pain realized.

The pastor looked at the letter, his expression tightening with unease. He whispered something to his board members, then asked for a moment. As they huddled across the room, a heavy silence filled the air. Minutes passed—each one thick with tension.

When they finally returned, their faces told the truth before their words did.

"Dr. Simpson," the pastor began softly, "we've made a deal with another church. We never intended to sell to you—we just needed your offer to push theirs higher. You understand—it's just business."

Those words pierced me like a blade to the chest.

This man had prayed with us, encouraged us when we struggled to get financing, and declared that God had spoken. We had worshiped there, held a baptism, and even performed a wedding. To us, it wasn't just a building—it was sacred space. It represented answered prayer.

He extended his hand in hollow apology, but I couldn't move. Every emotion collided within me—anger, grief, betrayal. My mind raced with everything I wanted to say, but before a single word escaped my lips, the Holy Spirit restrained me.

A stillness—divine and weighty—settled over me. I took a deep breath, looked at him, and simply said, "I see."

Then I turned and walked away.

THE WEIGHT OF LOSS

Outside, I stood in the parking lot holding the *Letter of Intent.* The bank president had finally approved our financing after months of prayer and meetings. We had overcome the impossible—only to be undone by deceit.

I looked at my wife—her eyes said everything. Then at the leaders who had accompanied me, the faithful ones who had prayed and believed beside me. The air felt heavy, the kind that presses faith to the edge of breaking.

"Every plan, every prayer, every ounce of faith may seem wasted right now," I said quietly, "but nothing catches God by surprise. He saw this coming long before we did—and He's already made provision for us."

They nodded, though disappointment shadowed their faces.

That night at home, my wife sat beside me—faith steady in her eyes even through heartache. "God's is going to work everything out in our favor," she said softly. "He's going to turn it around."

I echoed her words, praying they would echo back into my spirit: "*God's going to turn it around'.*

But deep down, I wrestled. *Had I missed God? Did I mishear His leading?*

THE AFTERMATH

When I told the congregation, the sanctuary fell into a heavy silence. You could feel the collective ache. Within weeks, half the board resigned, taking families and finances with them. People we had baptized, married, and discipled quietly drifted away.

Every departure reopened the wound.

Attendance dwindled. Finances dried up. In the natural, Faith Clinic—not yet five years old—appeared to be dying. Yet, in the midst of it all, a whisper rose in my heart:

"Do not place your faith in numbers. Keep trusting Me."

THE PAIN THAT STEELED UNITY

The pain touched every part of our lives, but none more deeply than our children. They were angry—not at God, but for our sake. Watching their parents hurt stirred something protective in them.

That night, we gathered the family and prayed. Our children—young adults then—made a covenant before God: to stand together, to protect the vision, to keep building what God started.

What began in sorrow became a sacred vow sealed in faith.

God was teaching us that sometimes unity is not born on the mountaintop, but in the valley. Brokenness became the cement that bound our hearts together.

THE BATTLE WITHIN

Even after the storm settled, I wrestled within. I prayed each morning, but something had shifted. The nearness I once felt seemed veiled. The Word was still powerful, but my joy in prayer felt faint.

I showed up—but I wasn't fully there. I ministered—but I was running on fumes.

Then, one morning before dawn, I stepped into my office. The room was still, dimly lit by the faint glow of streetlights. And in that stillness, I felt Him—waiting.

I sank to my knees, broken and weary, and whispered, "Lord... why?"

Why would You allow this? Why would You let our faith, our obedience, end in heartbreak?

As I think back, my questions and attitude sounded like an interrogation. But there was no rebuke, no explanation given, or comfort offered. Just silence.

The silence was deafening.

And then, in that silence, His presence filled the room—not with rebuke, but with tenderness.

"Do you trust Me?" He asked.

It wasn't an accusation; it was an invitation.

I hesitated. "Father, I want to... but I don't understand You right now."

Then, like a flood, memories began to surface—every miracle, every answered prayer, every moment He had carried me before. The grace. The anointing. The favor. The Holy Spirit was replaying God's faithfulness like a reel through my mind.

Then came His words again, soft yet piercing:

"You've trusted Me in blessing... will you trust Me in breaking?"

That question broke me open.

I fell to the floor and wept. "Father, I trust You—even when I don't understand. You are still my refuge, my fortress, my Abba."

And in that surrender, peace came. Quiet. Steady. Healing.

The pain didn't vanish—but it lost its power.

THE MINISTRY OF BROKENNESS

Looking back, that was one of the greatest altars of my life. God stripped away what I thought I needed so I could discover He was all I truly needed.

It wasn't punishment—it was preparation.

Prayer became my lifeline. I stopped asking God to change the storm and started asking Him to change me within it.

What I thought was rejection turned out to be redirection. What looked like a loss was actually protection.

Later I learned that the building we had pursued was riddled with hidden damage and major liabilities. Had we purchased it, it might have sunk our ministry during the recession that followed. God didn't withhold a blessing—He prevented a burden.

Sometimes, grace wears the disguise of disappointment.

And in that season, I learned something priceless: discernment is not the same as doubt. I had mistaken the Spirit's caution for fear. Now I know—when God checks your spirit, He's not denying your dream; He's directing your steps.

A few years later, God gave us a better building—with more land, more parking, and no debt. Glory to God!

Those who stayed became more than members—they became family. Their faithfulness became the backbone of our ministry. Together we learned that the greatest miracle of prayer isn't what God does *for* you—it's what He does *in* you.

A WORD TO THE WEARY

If you find yourself in a place that looks like loss—where prayer feels unanswered and trust feels hard to hold—know this: **God has not abandoned you.**

His silence is not absence. His delay is not denial. He is working in the shadows, shaping something in you that ease could never produce.

The same hands that allow the breaking are the hands that will heal and rebuild.

Your tears are not wasted—they water the soil of your future. Every prayer you've whispered in faith, even the ones soaked in doubt, has reached His heart.

When all you can do is whisper His name, that's enough. When you can't trace His hand, trust His heart. He's weaving purpose through your pain and preparing beauty from your ashes.

If you're standing where I once stood—confused, weary, and wondering if God still hears—He does. The same Presence that met me in that quiet, tear-soaked office will meet you where you are.

Let prayer become your lifeline. Not because it always changes what's around you—but because it always changes what's within you.

Reflection Questions

What has God allowed you to lose so He could teach you to rely fully on Him?

How do you respond when God's silence feels like absence?

In what area of your life do you need to release control and trust His sovereignty today?

Prayer

Father,

Thank You for the storms that reveal where my faith truly rests. When life feels uncertain, teach me to hold fast to You.

When betrayal wounds my heart, help me forgive as You have forgiven me. When resources run dry, remind me that You alone are my Source.

I choose to trust You—even when I don't understand, even when I can't see, even when I feel utterly alone.

Be my peace in the storm, my anchor in the deep, and my strength in the waiting.

In Jesus' name, Amen.

THE JOURNEY GOES DEEPER FROM HERE

When faith is tested, you discover something you can't learn in calm seasons: prayer is not just a habit... it's a lifeline. It becomes the place where you breathe again, where you steady your heart, where you lay your fears before God and refuse to let go of what He promised. In testing seasons, faith stops being something you "have" and becomes something you *lean on*.

But there is another dimension you step into when you refuse to quit—when you keep showing up in prayer even while tears are drying on your face, even while the answer hasn't arrived yet. Something begins to rise inside you that didn't exist before. It's subtle at first, but unmistakable.

Your language changes.

You stop praying from uncertainty and begin praying out of conviction. You stop rehearsing the problem and start declaring the promise.

You stop echoing what you feel and start speaking what God has already said.

That shift does not come from excitement... it comes from endurance. It's the fruit of standing your ground when everything in you wanted to walk away. And as that shift takes root, something powerful emerges—something that shakes both heaven and hell.

Your voice gains a tone of faith.

A believer who has been tested and still chooses to trust does not speak timidly. The trials that were meant to silence you actually train you. The storm that tried to break you become the very thing that forged your confidence in God.

And that is where the next chapter meets you—not in weakness, but in strength that was birthed through battle:

The Voice of Faith.

CHAPTER 12

PRAYING WITH AUTHORITY

Years ago, a man who was a member of my church came to see me after losing his job. He was a husband and father of two young children—let's call him a man named Mark. When he walked into my office, his shoulders were slumped, his eyes weary. He sat across from me and said quietly, "Pastor, I don't know what to do. I've sent out applications everywhere. My wife's worried, the bills are piling up, and I feel like I've failed my family."

I could hear the weight of fear and disappointment in his voice. After a moment, I said, "Mark, I know this season feels uncertain, but listen to me—you have to see beyond where you are. What you see in mind, you will see in time. You need to visualize by faith what you desire, then verbalize it with your mouth. When you do so, you're releasing faith for its manifestation."

He looked up, puzzled. "You mean I should just say it until it happens?"

I smiled and said, "Not just say it—believe it. Speak from your position in Christ, not from the conditions around you. You're not speaking wishful words; you're speaking truth from your seat of authority. God has already promised to supply all your needs. Your job now is to align your words with His Word."

We prayed together, and I told him to declare every morning, "I thank

You, Lord, that doors of provision are opening for me. The right opportunity is already prepared."

Two weeks later, that man came back with a light in his eyes I hadn't seen before. "Pastor," he said, "you won't believe it—a company I never even applied to called me. They said someone recommended me for a position. I start next week—better pay, better hours, better benefits!"

I smiled and said, "I do believe it. You didn't just find a job—you activated your faith."

He nodded, tears in his eyes. "You were right, Pastor. When I started seeing it in faith and speaking it out, peace replaced my panic. I stopped praying from fear and started praying from my position."

Listen, friend, faith doesn't deny the problem—it declares the promise. When you visualize by faith and verbalize with authority, heaven moves, and what you see in your spirit manifests in your life.

Why, because you are praying with authority. And that's what I am sharing with you in this chapter.

PRAYING FROM YOUR IDENTITY

When you truly know who you are in Christ, something awakens in your spirit. You stop praying as one pleading for access and start praying as one who already belongs. You no longer beg God to move—you learn to move in step with what He's already finished. Prayer becomes less about asking and more about aligning. It shifts from desperation to declaration, from hoping to knowing.

Ephesians 2:6 says, "God raised us up together, and made us sit together in the heavenly places in Christ Jesus." You are not trying to climb into His presence—you're already seated there. That seat is your place of authority, your position of rest. It's where your spirit stands tall even when life tries to bow you low.

When you pray from that seat, your perspective changes. You stop looking up at your battles and start looking down on them from heaven's point of view. You realize that your prayers don't have to fight their way to heaven—they start in heaven and speak into the earth. You're not praying toward victory anymore; you're praying from it.

PRAYING FROM POSITION, NOT PRESSURE

There's a difference between praying to get God's attention and praying knowing you already have it. Too often, believers pray from a place of pressure—out of fear, anxiety, or urgency—hoping their tears will convince God to intervene. But authority in prayer isn't born from emotion; it's born from identity.

When you pray from pressure, your words carry worry. But when you pray from position, your words carry weight. You stop saying, "Lord, if You can," and start declaring, "Lord, You already have." Because the cross didn't just save you—it repositioned you.

We now sit in heavenly places and are to pray from our seat of authority. That means you pray from your position, not your conditions. You don't let circumstances dictate your confidence; you let your covenant define it. You are not a beggar hoping for mercy—you are a son or daughter enforcing heaven's verdict on earth.

When you know where you're seated, fear loses its grip. You stop praying from the ground of defeat and start speaking from the throne of dominion. Heaven responds when you speak from where you're seated, not from where you struggle.

THE POWER OF AGREEMENT

Jesus said, "I will give you the keys of the kingdom of heaven, and whatever you bind on earth will be bound in heaven, and whatever you loose on earth will be loosed in heaven." (Matthew 16:19 NKJV) Those keys represent divine authority—heaven's permission for you to act on its behalf. Binding and loosing are not mystical concepts; they are legal terms. To bind means to forbid on earth what heaven has already forbidden. To loose means to release on earth what heaven has already declared free.

You're not ordering God—you're agreeing with Him. You're not giving heaven instructions—you're enforcing its decrees. When you declare His Word, heaven recognizes its own voice coming through you. Agreement gives your prayer authority, because heaven always honors its covenant.

Authority flows where alignment is found. The more your heart mirrors His, the more your words mirror His will.

THE AUTHORITY OF SPOKEN WORDS

Creation began with a voice: "Then God said, 'Let there be light'; and there was light." (Genesis 1:3 NKJV) The universe was shaped by a spoken word—and it still responds to one. The same Spirit that spoke light into darkness lives in you.

Proverbs 18:21 says, "Death and life are in the power of the tongue." That word power means authority. Your tongue carries jurisdiction in the Spirit. When you speak in faith, you release heaven's reality into earthly situations.

When Jesus healed, He spoke. When He rebuked storms, He spoke. When He cast out demons, He spoke. Heaven moves on the frequency of faith-filled words. Your words, when aligned with God's will, can release healing into pain, peace into panic, and hope into despair.

You can't create what heaven hasn't willed—but you can release what heaven has already finished. That's the beauty of authority in prayer—it declares eternal truth until it manifests in time.

FAITH THAT STANDS ITS GROUND

Authority without faith is just noise. Faith is what gives your words weight. It's the confidence that God's Word still governs your world, even when the storm rages.

Authority without intimacy becomes empty. Even Jesus, after miracles that shook the earth, withdrew to pray. Because the power that flows through you must always return to the Presence that fills you.

Jesus modeled this perfectly. In Mark 4:39, He stood in a storm and said, "Peace, be still." He didn't scream to overpower the waves—He spoke from rest. The peace within Him overruled the chaos around Him. That's what authority looks like—peace commanding panic, calm confronting chaos.

That same Spirit now lives in you. So when fear rises and life trembles, don't abandon your position. Stand firm. Speak what heaven has said, not what fear is shouting. Faith doesn't beg God to move—it believes He already has. It prays, not for victory, but from it.

WHEN AUTHORITY IS TESTED

Every believer who walks in authority will be tested. The enemy knows he's defeated, but he also knows that most believers don't act like it. That's why he uses deception—he wants to make you forget your position and surrender your confidence.

He whispered to Eve, "Has God indeed said...?" (Genesis 3:1 NKJV) and he whispers to you, "Are you sure you're worthy? Are you sure God's listening?" The enemy can't take your authority, but he'll do anything to make you doubt it.

Jesus faced the same attack in the wilderness. Yet He didn't argue—He declared: "It is written." Every time He spoke the Word, the enemy lost ground. That's your pattern too. When lies rise, speak truth. When fear strikes, declare faith. When doubt screams, answer with Scripture. You don't fight for victory—you stand in it until resistance breaks.

SPIRITUAL WARFARE

When you awaken to who you are in Christ, the atmosphere around you shifts. Heaven recognizes your authority—and so does hell. Prayer stops being comfortable and becomes confrontational. You begin reclaiming ground the enemy thought was his. But you never fight alone.

The Commander of Heaven's armies stands beside you. The Word of God is your weapon. The Spirit within you is your strength. Victory isn't something you chase—it's something you enforce.

So take your seat. Lift your voice. Speak heaven's words into earth's chaos. Because when you pray from your position, all of heaven stands behind your declaration.

KINGDOM IDENTITY AND ROYAL RESPONSIBILITY

Authority isn't about dominance—it's about representation. You're not here to prove power; you're here to reflect heaven. Scripture says, "We are ambassadors for Christ, as though God were pleading through us." (2 Corinthians 5:20 NKJV)

An ambassador doesn't speak their opinion—they declare their ruler's decree. That's the essence of prayer. It's not your will trying to persuade God; it's His will flowing through you. Authority is humility wearing confidence, because it knows who sent it.

When you walk in that understanding, heaven flows naturally through your words. You no longer strive to be powerful—you simply stay aligned with the One who is.

REFLECTION QUESTIONS

Do you find yourself praying under pressure or from your position in Christ?

What battles in your life need heaven's authority spoken over them?

How can you remind yourself daily that you're seated with Christ above every circumstance?

PRAYER

Father, thank You for seating me with Christ in heavenly places. Help me to remember that I'm not fighting for victory, but from it. When fear tries to pull me down, lift my gaze back to where I'm seated—with You.

Teach me to speak what You've said and to pray from the peace of Your presence. Let my words carry heaven's authority, and my heart reflect Your will. When I bind, let it be what You've already forbidden. When I release, let it be what You've already promised. May my prayers echo Your power and my life reveal Your glory. In Jesus' name, Amen.

The Journey Continues:

You've just stepped into the revelation of praying with authority—no longer pleading with God from a position of weakness, but standing in the confidence of who you are in Him. You now understand that your voice carries weight in the Spirit, that heaven backs what God has spoken, and that prayer is not powerlessness... it is partnership.

But before you move forward, there is something you must be prepared for—not to discourage you, but to strengthen you.

Authority is not proven on the days when everything is easy.

Anyone can pray boldly when doors are flying open, when miracles are visible, and when your heart feels full of certainty. The real test begins when life pushes back, when the answers take longer than expected, when you can't feel anything, and when the battle seems to intensify right after you prayed in faith.

That is the crossroads where many believers quietly grow discouraged—not because they lack faith, but because no one told them that faith is often refined in fire. The enemy will try to convince you that delay is denial, that silence means God has forgotten you, and that the promise is slipping away.

But that is a lie.

If the warfare increased, it is because something in your life has shifted in the spirit. Your prayers are working. Hell doesn't fight what isn't a threat.

This is where authority becomes more than a teaching.

This is where prayer becomes more than a discipline.

This is where your relationship with God becomes your anchor rather than a routine.

And that is the doorway to the next phase of this journey—one every believer must eventually walk through, not with fear, but with understanding:

When Faith Is Tested: Prayer Becomes a Lifeline.

CHAPTER 13

THE VOICE OF FAITH: SPEAKING WHAT HEAVEN HAS DECLARED

The sun had barely risen when I stepped outside. The air was crisp, still carrying the chill of dawn. As I walked the familiar path down the walking trails near my house, I noticed how the first light touched the leaves—turning dew into diamonds. It was quiet except for the faint chorus of morning birds.

And in that stillness, I heard a whisper within my spirit: "Speak what you believe, not what you see."

Faith, I realized, has a voice.

It isn't loud or boastful—it's steady. It speaks when everything else falls silent. It declares that when nothing has changed yet. It believes before the evidence appears.

That morning, I wasn't just walking through nature; I was walking through revelation.

Faith is not silence—it's sound.

When God created the world, He didn't think light into existence; He spoke it. "Then God said, 'Let there be light'; and there was light" (Genesis 1:3, NKJV). Creation began with a declaration. Heaven responded to the sound of divine faith.

And because you were made in His image, your words carry creative power too. But that power is not born from emotion—it's born from identity. You must speak not from the weight of your circumstances but from the strength of your position as a child of God.

When this becomes real, your prayers shift. You stop echoing fear and start declaring your Father's truth. You stop rehearsing what the enemy said and start repeating what heaven has decreed.

The language of faith always sounds like agreement—it aligns with heaven's verdict even when earth hasn't caught up yet.

FAITH SPEAKS FROM REVELATION, NOT REACTION

Most people pray from reaction—they respond to trouble, pain, or fear. But faith speaks from revelation—it responds to truth. Faith listens first to what God says, then echoes it back into the atmosphere.

When David faced Goliath, he didn't rehearse the size of his enemy; he proclaimed the greatness of his God. While others described the problem, David decreed the promise. His words carried weight because they were born from intimacy, not insecurity.

That's the difference between wishful thinking and faith-filled speaking. Faith doesn't try to manipulate outcomes—it manifests agreement.

Jesus said, "Whoever says to this mountain, 'Be removed and be cast into the sea,' and does not doubt in his heart, but believes that those things he says will be done, he will have whatever he says" (Mark 11:23, NKJV).

Notice—He didn't say, Whoever believes silently. He said, whoever says. Faith is expressed through sound. Heaven moves when earth agrees.

ABRAHAM'S ECHO

Abraham understood this truth. God called him "the father of many nations" before he even had a son. Scripture says Abraham "did not waver at the promise of God through unbelief, but was strengthened in faith, giving glory to God" (Romans 4:20, NKJV).

He believed before he saw. He spoke life into barrenness. His faith was not passive—it was prophetic.

Every time Abraham looked at the stars, he saw promises that hadn't yet appeared. When Sarah laughed in doubt, Abraham kept declaring what God had said. His words were building a future that his eyes could not yet see.

That's what faith does—it speaks into the void until life fills it. It proclaims healing while sickness still lingers. It declares peace while storms still rage. It calls things that are not as though they already were.

Faith doesn't deny reality; it defies its final say.

DAVID AT ZIKLAG: WHEN FAITH FINDS ITS VOICE

There is perhaps no clearer picture of the voice of faith than David at Ziklag.

He returned from battle to find the unimaginable. The city was burned. Smoke still rose from the ruins. The homes were gone. Their goods were plundered. The families of David and his men had all been taken captive.

Everything familiar had been touched by loss.

David lost his family.

He lost his property.

He almost lost the trust of his men.

The same warriors who had once stood beside him now wept until they had no more power to weep. Grief turned into bitterness, and talk of stoning David began to rise among them (see 1 Samuel 30). He was surrounded by sorrow, surrounded by anger, surrounded by what looked like the worst failure of his life.

This was more than a bad day. It was a defining day.

In that moment of pain, grief, and loss, David had a choice: agree with what he saw, or return to what he knew about God.

I believe David remembered the God who had been with him in earlier battles—the God who gave him courage to face a lion, a bear, and a giant. He hadn't survived those moments because he was gifted. He survived because God was with him.

Scripture says, "But David strengthened himself in the Lord his God" (1 Samuel 30:6, NKJV).

How does a man do that when his world is on fire?

I believe David did what we have been learning: he began not with petition, but with adoration. I imagine him, even with tears still in his eyes, turning his heart toward the One who had never failed him. Before he asked for directions, he returned to devotion.

He called for the ephod. That was not just a ritual act; it was a posture. It meant, "I am going to seek the Lord." And I believe he did it the way he always had—through stillness, through worship, through remembering who God is.

He didn't rush straight to "What should I do?"
First, he turned his attention to "Who are You?"

There, in the ashes of Ziklag, David lifted his heart in adoration. He honored God's faithfulness in his past. He worshiped the God who had delivered him before. And out of that place of reverence, he inquired:

"Shall I pursue this troop? Shall I overtake them?" (1 Samuel 30:8,

NKJV).

Petition came after adoration. Request followed reverence.

Then heaven answered.

"And He answered him, 'Pursue, for you shall surely overtake them and without fail recover all'" (1 Samuel 30:8, NKJV).

Once David received that word, something shifted. The man who had just wept in the dust now stood in the strength of a promise. I believe David rose from that encounter and, with the voice of faith, declared in his spirit and to his men, "We will pursue the enemy—and we will recover all."

His men had been ready to stone him, but the sound of faith changed the atmosphere. David's confidence in God became contagious. His voice of faith gave his weary men faith for the battle.

They went.

They fought.

And they did exactly what heaven had already declared—they recovered all that had been taken and took possession of their enemies' goods.

This is what the voice of faith does. It hears what God has spoken in the secret place of adoration, then declares it in the face of loss. It turns devastated warriors into determined pursuers. It moves a broken leader from despair to declaration.

Faith doesn't ignore ruin. It speaks into ruins with the word of the Lord.

YOUR POSITION DETERMINES YOUR VOICE

To speak with faith, you must pray from your position—not your condition.

Conditions change. Circumstances fluctuate. Feelings rise and fall. But your position in Christ never moves.

You are seated with Him in heavenly places. You are covered by His righteousness, surrounded by His promises, and sustained by His Spirit.

When you speak from that place—when you open your mouth as a child of God rather than a slave to fear—your words carry the authority of your Father's throne.

Faith is not wishful thinking; it's positional speaking.

When you declare the Word of God, you're echoing heaven's decree. You're not trying to convince God to act—you're partnering with what He has already established.

That's why Jesus could sleep in the storm. He wasn't governed by the winds of circumstance but by the authority of His position. And when He spoke, creation obeyed its Creator.

Faith-filled speech is not arrogance—it's alignment. It's when your heart says, "Let it be to me according to Your word."

WHEN FAITH TREMBLES BUT STILL SPEAKS

There will be moments when doubt whispers louder than faith—when your words feel hollow and your prayers seem unanswered. But remember this: faith speaks even when it trembles.

The centurion in Matthew 8 understood this power. He told Jesus, "Just say the word, and my servant will be healed." His confidence wasn't in proximity but in authority. He recognized that when Jesus spoke, heaven moved.

That same authority now abides in you through His Spirit.

When you speak His Word, mountains listen. When you declare His promises, demons scatter. When you align your voice with His, impossible situations begin to shift.

Faith doesn't always roar; sometimes it whispers. But even a whisper, when rooted in truth, can shake hell. Heaven doesn't respond to panic—it responds to faith.

THE SEED THAT SPEAKS

Faith-filled words are not just declarations—they are divine seeds.

Every time you speak God's truth, you plant something eternal. You may not see the harvest immediately, but heaven does. The ground of prayer always produces when the seed of faith is sown.

Jesus said, "If you have faith as a mustard seed, you can say to this mountain, 'Move from here to there,' and it will move" (Matthew 17:20, NKJV).

Notice again—He didn't say you think to the mountain. He said you are to speak to it.

Because faith doesn't stay silent—it speaks in alignment with the One who never lies.

You may not feel powerful when you pray, but your words carry the DNA of heaven when they agree with God's Word. Every declaration becomes a seed sown in the soil of time, watered by perseverance, and harvested in due season.

Your "Let there be" may sound small today, but one day it will stand as testimony to what faith birthed through your voice.

THE BATTLE BETWEEN SIGHT AND SOUND

Faith and sight are often at war. Sight reports what is; faith declares what will be. Sight says, "It's over." Faith says, "It's just beginning."

Sight observes; faith obeys.

When you pray, you must decide which one will have authority—your eyes or your ears. "So then faith comes by hearing, and hearing by the word of God" (Romans 10:17, NKJV).

Faith doesn't come by seeing; it comes by hearing—and then by speaking what was heard. That's why the enemy attacks your confession: if he can silence your sound, he can stall your breakthrough.

Your voice is the bridge between revelation and manifestation. When you speak God's Word, you give shape to what heaven has already authorized.

KEEP SPEAKING

So keep speaking. Even when the night feels long and the evidence is absent, keep declaring what heaven has already written over your life.

Speak healing where there is pain.
Speak peace where there is fear.
Speak hope where there is despair.
Speak victory where there seems to be none.

When you speak from your position as a child, you release heaven's authority on earth.

And when you speak in agreement—with heaven, with Scripture, and with your brothers and sisters in faith—you amplify heaven's sound through your voice.

Faith doesn't just wait—it works through words. It doesn't just believe silently—it believes aloud.

So open your mouth and speak. Speak to your mountain. Speak over your family. Speak to your destiny. Heaven is waiting for the sound of your faith.

Reflection Questions

Are your words shaped by what you see or by what God has said?

How can you begin praying and declaring from your position as a child of God rather than from your current situation?

What promises from Scripture do you need to start speaking daily until they take root in your heart?

Where do you see yourself in David's story at Ziklag—surrounded by loss, strengthening yourself in the Lord, or declaring, "I will recover all"?

Prayer

Father,

Let my voice echo heaven. Teach me to speak from faith, not fear—from my position, not my pain. Help me declare Your Word with confidence and consistency. Let every word that leaves my lips agree with what You've already decreed. When I speak, let heaven move. When I pray, let faith rise. Make my mouth a vessel of truth and my tongue an instrument of victory. In Jesus' name, Amen.

Coming Next: The Manifestation of the Prayer of Faith

When faith finds its voice, it sets miracles in motion. But when that voice meets obedience—when prayer is matched with action—the invisible becomes visible. The next chapter unveils how heaven's decrees manifest through believing hearts and obedient steps.

CHAPTER 14

THE MANIFESTATION OF FAITH AND PRAYER

THE POWER THAT PRAYER RELEASES

The night was still. Only the low hum of the air conditioner and the ticking of the clock filled the room. My office light cast a soft glow across the walls, and my Bible lay open where I had left it hours earlier. I wasn't praying with words anymore—I was simply sitting in His presence, listening. It was the kind of silence that isn't empty, but full—full of expectancy, full of the awareness that Heaven was near.

It had been months since that day outside the church property—the day I held a check in my hand and called it loss. In that moment, disappointment felt heavy and final. But Heaven had called it something else—preparation. God hadn't denied me; He had been aligning me. What I thought was rejection had really been redirection. Prayer hadn't rescued me from the storm; it had reshaped me in it. And somewhere in that reshaping, I discovered a quiet strength—the kind that doesn't roar, but remains.

That night, I leaned back in my chair and whispered, "Father, thank You for not giving me what I wanted... because You were preparing me for what I needed."

The words felt unfamiliar at first, but they carried weight. As they left my lips, revelation began to fill the room. The Holy Spirit started to show me that alignment is the atmosphere where miracles are born. God's will had never stopped moving—it was waiting for me to move with it. Prayer, I realized, isn't about convincing God to act; it's about agreeing with what He has already decided. When faith and the Word align, Heaven manifests on earth.

My eyes drifted to the open Bible in front of me. They fell on James 5:16: "The effective, fervent prayer of a righteous man avails much." I had quoted that verse for years—preached it, taught it, believed it. But that night, one word came alive—effective.

Then, in that gentle way I've come to recognize, I heard the whisper of the Holy Spirit: "Prayer becomes effective when the one praying is in alignment."

That phrase unlocked everything that followed.

I began to understand that miracles are not random acts of mercy; they are the fruit of divine agreement. When your faith, your words, and your prayers line up with the Word of God, you create a conduit through which Heaven can manifest on earth. Jesus taught us to pray, "Your kingdom come. Your will be done on earth as it is in heaven." That was not poetic language—it was a prophetic blueprint for manifestation.

Faith is Heaven's language, and prayer is the voice that speaks it. When you pray from alignment, not emotion—from your position, not your condition—you give God room to perform what He has already promised. Heaven is always ready to move; it waits for agreement on earth.

That night, I realized God had been ready all along—ready to lead me into miracle manifestation, ready to release what had been held back by misalignment. He didn't need me to pray louder; He needed me to pray truer. To come into harmony with His Word so His will could flow unhindered.

Sitting there in that quiet room, surrounded by peace and promise, I whispered one more prayer: "Father, align my heart with Your Word. Let my faith echo Heaven until Your will is seen on earth. Lead me into what You've already prepared."

In that moment, the air felt charged—not just with peace, but with power. Because alignment always precedes manifestation. Heaven was ready to move.

THE KEY TO PRAYING EFFECTIVE PRAYERS

The key to praying effective prayers is to identify God's will and align your petitions with it. John said it plainly:

"Now this is the confidence that we have in Him, that if we ask anything according to His will, He hears us. And if we know that He hears us, whatever we ask, we know that we have the petitions that we have asked of Him" (1 John 5:14–15, NKJV).

Saving, healing, delivering—these are not occasional acts of mercy; they are the very will of God. All a believer must do is align with that will—declaring by faith that God saves, heals, and delivers all who believe and receive His promises.

I knew I believed, but I also realized that believing alone was not enough. Faith had to be activated. When people came to Jesus, they didn't come to test Him; they came because they knew He could heal them.

In Matthew 9, two blind men followed Him, crying out for mercy:

"And when He had come into the house, the blind men came to Him. And Jesus said to them, 'Do you believe that I am able to do this?' They said to Him, 'Yes, Lord.' Then He touched their eyes, saying, 'According to your faith let it be to you.' And their eyes were opened" (Matthew 9:28–30, NKJV).

That passage became living truth to me. My assignment as a pastor was not merely to pray for the sick—it was to help build their faith to receive what God had already made available. My role was to align their faith with the Word through teaching and the anointing.

That revelation changed everything.

Prayer was never meant to persuade God; it was meant to partner with Him. When our faith aligns with His Word, Heaven begins to manifest His will on earth.

WHEN HEAVEN MOVES THROUGH ALIGNMENT

One Sunday night during service, after my wife and I had fasted and prayed for a supernatural move of God, I began preaching on The God Who Still Heals, Delivers, and Works Miracles. I could sense the tangible presence of the Lord in the room—the power of God to heal and restore hovered like a mantle over the people. But I knew I had to keep preaching until faith aligned with that power.

That is what Jesus did in Luke 5. Scripture says, "Now it happened on a certain day, as He was teaching, that there were Pharisees and teachers of the law sitting by... And the power of the Lord was present to heal them" (Luke 5:17, NKJV).

The power to heal was present, yet no one received—until four men tore through a roof and lowered their paralyzed friend before Jesus. They didn't need healing themselves, but they had faith for someone else's miracle. Scripture says, "When Jesus saw their faith..." and in that moment, healing manifested.

That night at our church, something similar unfolded.

A cowboy walked in—quiet, rugged, wearing a tight bandage wrapped around his chest. He had been kicked by a horse, and several ribs were shattered. Every breath was agony. He and his wife were desperate; they had no medical insurance, no savings, and no backup plan.

As I preached, I felt faith rising in the room. When I called for those who needed healing, they hesitated at first. Then, as the presence of God swept through the sanctuary, they stepped forward. People were being touched everywhere—pain leaving, tears flowing, joy breaking out.

When I reached them, the cowboy began unbuttoning his shirt, revealing the thick wrapping around his ribs. His wife, tearful and trembling, said softly, "Pastor, he's been in constant pain. We've prayed, but tonight... we're believing."

I smiled and asked, "Do you believe God can heal you?"

Without hesitation, they both answered, "Yes." His wife added, "We gave our lives to Christ here last month. I know the same God who saved us can heal him tonight."

I placed one hand on his head and the other on his chest. "Be healed, in Jesus' name."

Instantly, his face flushed red. He gasped and began to twist from side to side. I stepped back and said, "Press where it hurt."

He did—and there was no pain.

The sunken ribs had completely lifted. Right there in front of everyone, he tore off the bandage and let out a cowboy yell that echoed through the sanctuary. His wife dropped to her knees, weeping as the congregation erupted in praise.

When I handed him the microphone, he said, "When you touched me, I felt heat go through my ribs—and then I felt them move back into place. I just knew I was healed!"

That night, God didn't just heal broken ribs—He restored faith, hope, and provision to a struggling family. It was a visible demonstration of divine alignment: faith met the Word, prayer met power, and Heaven manifested the will of God on earth.

REFLECTION QUESTIONS

What prayer have you been believing God for that requires you to stand in faith rather than strive in fear?

How has God used waiting seasons to strengthen your trust and shape your character?

Are there actions of obedience He's prompting you to take that align with what you've already prayed?

When you look back, can you identify moments when what seemed like delay was actually divine preparation?

How can you turn your next answered prayer into a testimony that glorifies God and strengthens others' faith?

PRAYER – THE MANIFESTATION OF FAITH AND PRAYER

Father, thank You for being faithful to every word You have spoken. When my eyes cannot see, teach my heart to still believe. Let my prayers be rooted in Your promises, not my emotions. Help me to act in faith, speak in faith, and wait in faith—knowing that every word You've declared is already settled in Heaven. Strengthen me when the waiting feels long and remind me that Your silence is not absence but preparation. Breathe fresh courage into my spirit, that I may trust You without wavering and praise You without proof. Manifest Your will in my life according to Your perfect timing, and let every answered prayer reflect Your glory and love. In Jesus' name, Amen.

Faith brings manifestation—but manifestation isn't the end of prayer; it's the beginning of something deeper. Once you've tasted the power of answered prayer, the question becomes: How do you keep that fire burning?

Many celebrate the breakthrough but neglect the altar that birthed it. True faith doesn't stop at receiving—it continues in relationship. There is a fire that sustains what faith begins: the inner life of prayer, the secret flame that keeps you aligned when the noise of the world fades.

In the next chapter, we will step behind the veil to discover the secret fire that turns prayer from a moment into a lifestyle.

CHAPTER 15

THE SECRET FIRE: SUSTAINING A LIFE OF PRAYER

The sanctuary was dark, illuminated only by the faint glow of the exit sign and a few lights plugged into the wall—each one casting a soft path that seemed to lead me toward the door, toward home. Everyone had left hours ago, yet I remained—sitting quietly on the steps of the altar, my Bible resting across my lap. The scent of anointing oil still lingered in the air. It had been one of those nights when heaven kissed the earth—miracles, tears, and worship mingled together like incense rising.

But sitting there in the stillness, I realized something deeper: the power of prayer isn't sustained by moments—it's sustained by intimacy. Miracles are born in encounters, but they are kept alive by communion. The same fire that ignites faith must be tended daily, or it will fade into memory.

I whispered softly, "Father, keep me burning."

It wasn't a request for more power—it was a cry for more presence. Because I had learned that what sustains a move of God isn't noise—it's nearness. The fire that roars in public must be refueled in private. That is where transformation becomes a way of life.

FROM MANIFESTATION TO MAINTENANCE

Many believers experience answered prayers but lose the discipline that birthed them. They shout at the miracle, yet walk away from the altar that made it possible. Manifestation was never meant to end prayer—it was meant to deepen it.

When God answers, it's not a finish line; it's an invitation. Every miracle is a doorway—an opening into deeper intimacy. Faith for the breakthrough must mature into fellowship beyond the breakthrough. What you gain through prayer can only be sustained through prayer.

Jesus understood this rhythm. Even after the crowds saw miracles, He withdrew to lonely places to pray (Luke 5:16). Power didn't make Him less dependent on the Father—it brought Him closer. He wasn't chasing moments; He was maintaining communion. That is the pattern of the secret fire.

THE FIRE THAT MUST BE TENDED

In Leviticus 6:12–13, God gave a simple but powerful command:

"And the fire on the altar shall be kept burning on it; it shall not be put out... A fire shall always be burning on the altar; it shall never go out."

The priests didn't start the fire—that was God's doing. But they were responsible for keeping it alive.

That is the same responsibility every believer carries. God lights the flame when you encounter Him, but devotion keeps it burning. And that fire is more than emotion; it's alignment. It is the daily surrender that keeps you in rhythm with His will.

We often pray for fresh fire without realizing that fire does not fall on empty altars. God doesn't reignite what we've abandoned—He breathes on what we continually offer. The flame stays alive through faithfulness, not feelings.

THE SECRET PLACE: WHERE FIRE IS FED

The secret fire is fed in the secret place. It is there that alignment with the Word becomes more than knowledge—it becomes breath. No one carries sustained authority in public unless they carry sustained intimacy in private.

In the secret place, faith stops being situational and becomes relational. You stop measuring God's goodness by outcomes and start resting in His nature. You stop praying to get results and start praying to stay aligned.

Jesus said in Matthew 6:6, "When you pray, go into your room, and when you have shut your door, pray to your Father who is in the secret place; and your Father who sees in secret will reward you openly."

He didn't say if you pray, but when. The reward isn't only the answer—it's the awareness of His presence. When your secret life burns, your public life reflects His glory.

ALIGNMENT KEEPS THE FIRE ALIVE

There are seasons when prayer feels effortless, and seasons when prayer feels like work. But consistency shapes you. You don't always feel the flame, but if you remain aligned, the fire never dies.

Alignment with God's Word means you pray His will—and not just your wants. Scripture becomes your compass. You stop praying from the ground of emotion and start praying from the position of revelation.

The secret fire isn't fueled by striving—it is fed by surrender. It burns brighter when you yield instead of push, when you trust instead of panic. As your heart stays aligned, your life becomes an altar God keeps aflame.

The more you pray in faith, the more Heaven manifests its will through you. God doesn't just want to answer your prayers—He wants to make you an answer.

A LESSON FROM THE QUIET SEASON

I remember a season when I prayed daily for direction, yet Heaven seemed silent. Every door I tried to open closed before me. It felt like nothing was working—but something was.

God was aligning my desires with His will. He was quieting my striving so I could hear His whisper. That is the hidden work of the secret fire—it purifies the motives behind your prayers.

When I finally stopped pushing for my plan and started asking for His, everything shifted. Doors opened without effort. Provision came without pressure. Miracles began to flow where worry once lived.

I learned that the greatest manifestation of God's will doesn't come through loud faith—it comes through aligned faith. The kind of faith that listens more than it talks. The kind that burns in silence but glows in obedience.

FROM ALTAR TO ATMOSPHERE

When a fire burns within you, it changes what surrounds you. A believer aligned with Heaven carries an atmosphere. Peace walks in before you do. Authority follows every word you speak—not because you are powerful, but because you are positioned.

That is why alignment matters. When your heart burns with the Word, your prayers release Heaven's agenda into the earth. Your home becomes a dwelling of peace. Your workplace becomes a place of favor. Your words carry healing where pain once lived.

Every move of God begins in the heart of someone whose inner altar still burns. You don't need a platform—you need a flame.

GUARDING THE FIRE

Every fire faces opposition—distraction, disappointment, discouragement. The enemy knows that if he can't steal your faith, he'll try to smother your focus. That's why guarding your fire is essential.

Keep the Word before you. Worship even when it is quiet. Pray even when you don't feel it. Feed your spirit with what fuels the flame—truth, gratitude, surrender, and worship.

Guard your time with God as fiercely as you guard your breath. Because without the secret place, even the strongest believer can grow dim. But with it, even the weakest ember can spark revival.

THE FIRE THAT NEVER FADES

The longer I walk with God, the more I learn—fire does not always look like a blaze. Sometimes it is a quiet glow that refuses to die. Sometimes it is not shouting in tongues, but resting in trust.

That is the fire of alignment—the merging of your will with His until His desires become your rhythm. And when you live in that rhythm, prayer stops being an event and becomes an environment. You don't visit God's presence—you carry it.

REFLECTION QUESTIONS – THE FIRE THAT SUSTAINS FAITH

What does the "fire on the altar" look like in your daily walk with God? Are you tending the flame of your private devotion as faithfully as you celebrate public blessings?

What practices—Scripture, worship, solitude—help keep your heart aligned?

In what areas of your life is the Holy Spirit calling you back to intimacy? How can you turn answered prayers into lasting communion instead of momentary gratitude?

PRAYER — KEEP ME BURNING

Father, thank You for the fire You've placed within me. Teach me to tend it with faithfulness and love. When I'm tempted to rush ahead, slow me down to listen. When distractions crowd my mind, draw me into stillness. Keep my heart aligned with Your Word so that my prayers carry Your will. Let the flame of Your presence never fade within me. May every miracle I see only draw me closer to the One who performs it. Turn every answered prayer into deeper intimacy. Keep me burning—quietly, steadily, unshakably—for You.

In Jesus' name, Amen.

The fire of faith was never meant to flare and fade—it was meant to endure. It is the continual exchange between your surrender and His strength. The same Spirit who lights the flame will sustain it through every season... if you keep returning to the altar of alignment.

CHAPTER 16

THE BENEDICTION: A LIFE SHAPED BY PRAYER

As I reached the end of writing this book, I felt a gentle nudge to step away from my desk. I walked outside into the early October evening air, and to my surprise, it was perfectly calm—not too warm, not too cool, just still. The sun hung low, painting the horizon with strokes of gold and crimson. The breeze carried the scent of grass and earth, and somewhere beyond the trees, I could hear the faint laughter of children mingling with the whisper of the wind.

It was peaceful—but more than that; it was sacred. It felt like Heaven had drawn near, wrapping the evening in a quiet kind of glory. I stood there at the edge of my backyard—the same place where I had prayed countless times before—and suddenly, memories of this journey came flooding back: the early mornings of seeking, the nights of wrestling, the tears, the silence, and the breakthroughs.

Prayer had not simply been something I *did*; it had become who I *was*. Through every chapter, every word, every lesson, it had carved something eternal into me—a deeper dependence, a quieter strength, a steadier peace.

And as I stood there, breathing in the stillness, I thought of *you*.

Yes—you. The one who has walked with me through these pages. The one who paused, reflected, prayed, wept, and grew along the way. You didn't just read this book—you *journeyed* through it. You've sat in the same presence I've sat in, felt the same tug of the Spirit I've felt, and opened your heart to the same God who has been shaping mine.

And because of that, you are a part of this story.

You see, this isn't just my benediction—it's *ours*.

We've walked through valleys of silence and climbed the mountains of revelation together. We've seen that prayer isn't about performance—it's about presence. It's not about finding the right words—it's about finding His heart. It's the place where your story intertwines with His purpose, where the ordinary becomes holy, and where every whisper offered in faith carries eternal weight.

Prayer doesn't just change circumstances—it changes *you*. It teaches you humility in waiting, courage in warfare, and gratitude in blessing. It molds the heart until it beats in rhythm with Heaven's. And when your heart begins to move in that rhythm, everything shifts. You start walking slower, listening longer, loving deeper. You begin to see the world through the Father's eyes.

Jesus lived that way. His life was one unbroken prayer—a conversation that never ceased. Whether surrounded by crowds or alone in the wilderness, His heart was always turned toward the Father. He prayed before choosing the twelve, before healing the sick, before facing the cross. But He also prayed in moments of joy, lifting His eyes and saying, "Father, I thank You."

For Jesus, prayer wasn't a preparation for life—it *was* life. And that is the life He invites you into.

When prayer becomes the foundation of your days, you'll find peace in uncertainty, purpose in pain, and presence in the mundane. You'll discover that every answered prayer is a testimony, and every unanswered one is an invitation—to trust deeper, to love wider, to see higher.

Even the silence becomes sacred.

Because in prayer, nothing is ever wasted. Every sigh, every tear, every unspoken word becomes part of the conversation between your heart and His. Prayer weaves your life into the fabric of eternity.

Paul said it simply: *"Pray without ceasing."* He wasn't giving us a rule; he was showing us a rhythm—a way of life where every moment becomes communion. That's what a life shaped by prayer looks like. It's not defined by perfection, but by presence. You learn to rise and rest in His will, to speak and stay silent in His wisdom, to rejoice and to weep in His strength.

And here's the beautiful truth: prayer doesn't end with "Amen." It continues with every breath you take.

The greatest legacy of a praying life isn't found in the miracles you witness—it's found in the intimacy you cultivate. It's not measured by the number of answers, but by the depth of relationship. It's not proven by power alone, but by peace that endures.

When you live this way—when prayer becomes your home—you begin to resemble the One you commune with. His compassion becomes your compassion. His voice becomes your tone. His peace becomes your presence. You begin to carry His fragrance into every room you enter, until prayer isn't just what you *offer*—it's what you *carry*.

And so, this is our benediction of prayer:

That our hearts become living altars.

That our words become seeds of faith.

That our silence becomes sacred ground.

That our lives become unending conversations with the Father who loves us.

May every prayer you've ever prayed lead you closer to His heart.

May every unanswered question draw you deeper into His trust.

And may your final breath on this earth be like your first one in eternity—a prayer rising into the presence of the One who has always listened.

Because prayer was never just for this life—it's the language of the next.

Before you turn this final page, I want to thank you personally—for purchasing this book, for opening your heart, and for allowing me to walk with you through this sacred journey. Writing these words has been an act of obedience, but reading them—that was *your* act of faith.

I have prayed for you as I've written. I've asked God to meet you in every line, to heal where you've been wounded, to strengthen what has grown weary, and to set ablaze the flame of prayer within your heart. And I believe He has—and He will.

I look forward with great joy to the changes this journey will bring in your life—the deepened intimacy, the renewed fire, the miracles that will unfold as you continue to pray from your position of victory, not your place of struggle.

And if you've come this far and realize you've never fully surrendered your life to Jesus Christ—then this next moment is for you. Turn the page. There, you'll find *The Prayer of Salvation*—an invitation to begin the greatest conversation of your life.

Because prayer doesn't end here.

This is where it truly begins—again.

THE PRAYER OF SALVATION

RECEIVE A NEW LIFE AND A NEW BEGING

This is your moment—the sacred intersection between surrender and new beginnings. You don't have to have all the answers or be perfect. You just have to be honest. God loves you, and He's been waiting for this very moment to meet you right where you are.

You've spent time trying to fix what's broken, to fill the emptiness, to make sense of the pain. But peace isn't found in striving—it's found in surrender. The Father's arms are open, not to punish, but to embrace. He has seen your tears, your fears, and your struggles, and still, He calls you by name. From the day you were born, His love has been reaching for you. And now—right now—He's inviting you to begin again.

If you're ready to turn from the old and step into new life, pray these words—not from your lips alone, but from your heart.

PRAYER

Father God, I come to You today because I need You. I've tried to live life my way, and it hasn't worked. I believe that Jesus is Your Son—that He died for me and rose again so that I can have new life.

Lord Jesus, I open my heart to You. Please forgive me for every wrong I've done. Wash away my guilt, my shame, and the pain of my past. Make me new on the inside and help me live a life that honors You.

Jesus, I receive You as my Lord and Savior. I believe right now that I am forgiven and saved. **Holy Spirit,** fill me with Your presence. Give me strength to walk in truth, courage to follow You, and peace to remind me I am never alone.

Father, from this moment on, my life belongs to You. Lead me, guide me, and help me grow closer to You each day. Thank You for loving me, forgiving me, and saving me.

In Jesus' name, Amen.

NOW THAT YOU'RE SAVED: THE FIRST STEPS OF FAITH

Welcome home. You've just made the most life-changing decision of your life. Heaven is rejoicing because you said "yes" to God.

"There is joy in the presence of the angels of God over one sinner who repents." — *Luke 15:10 (NKJV)*

Salvation isn't an ending—it's a beginning. You've been born again, not into religion, but into relationship. The same Spirit that raised Jesus from the dead now lives within you. He will walk with you, speak to you, and never leave you. This is the beginning of your journey—learning to hear His voice, grow in His Word, and walk in His love.

1. TALK TO GOD EVERY DAY

Prayer is the breath of your new life. Don't worry about sounding perfect—God listens to the language of the heart. Speak to Him openly. Thank Him for saving you. Ask Him for wisdom, peace, and strength. He's not distant; He's closer than your next breath.

2. READ YOUR BIBLE

The Word of God is your nourishment. It reveals who He is—and who you are in Him. Start with the Gospel of John. Let His truth anchor you when life feels uncertain. The Word will teach you to walk in victory and remind you daily that you are never alone.

3. FIND A CHURCH FAMILY

You were not designed to walk alone. Find a Spirit-filled, Bible-believing church where you can grow, serve, and belong. Faith strengthens in fellowship. When you gather with others, God's presence multiplies among you.

4. BE WATER BAPTIZED

Baptism is your declaration to the world that you belong to Christ. When you go under the water, it symbolizes your old life being buried. When you rise again, it declares that you've been raised to new life in Jesus.

5. INVITE THE HOLY SPIRIT TO FILL YOU

The Holy Spirit is not an experience; He is a Person. He's your Comforter, Teacher, and Guide. He gives you power to pray, courage to stand, and grace to live righteously. Ask Him to fill you daily, and your walk will overflow with His peace and purpose.

6. SHARE YOUR STORY

Your story is light for someone still walking in darkness. Tell others what Jesus has done for you. You may not realize it yet, but your testimony carries power—the power to awaken hope in others.

A Gift For You

I have an eBook for new believers called *"The Walk of Faith."* It's my gift to you. This resource has helped many first-time believers—and those who've returned—to grow strong in their walk with God. You'll learn about His plan for your life and how to live with confidence and joy as a follower of Christ.

To receive your free copy, email **faithclinic77@gmail.com** and ask for *"The Salvation Book."*

Welcome to the family of God—where your new life has just begun.

ACKNOWLEDGEMENTS

I want to express my love and gratitude to my wife, Pat, for her unwavering love, encouragement, and steadfast support throughout the writing of this book. You have been my rock, my partner, and my inspiration every step of the way, and I am eternally grateful for you.

A special thanks to my children—Darius, Dereik, LaKisha, Jerriel, and Tommy—for your love, support, and belief in me. Each of you brings joy and strength to my life, and your encouragement has been a source of motivation and pride.

To the members and supporters of Faith Clinic Christian Center, my heartfelt thanks to each of you for your prayers, encouragement, and un-wavering faith in this mission. Your support has been invaluable, and this book came to fruition with you by my side.

To all who have walked this journey with me—thank you for being part of my life and for inspiring me to give my best in everything I do. I am deeply grateful.

With love and appreciation,
D. Lee A, Simpson

AUTHOR'S OTHER BOOKS

"TRANSFORMATION: CHANGE BEGINS WITHIN — THE JOURNEY TO YOUR BEST SELF"

Your best life doesn't begin when circumstances change — it begins when you change. Deep within you is a version of you that God designed with purpose, power, and potential. This book is your invitation to discover that person.

Transformation: Change Begins Within — The Journey To Your Best Self equips you with the spiritual keys needed to overcome what has held you back and step forward into who God created you to be. Through biblical truth, relatable stories, and simple daily applications, you'll learn how to:

• Renew your mind to think with clarity and faith • Break cycles of negativity, fear, and self-limiting beliefs • Embrace how God sees you — loved, chosen, and capable • Develop habits that support lasting spiritual and emotional growth • Live with bold expectation and walk confidently in your purpose

Each chapter guides you through a process of inner change — a journey from the pain of your past into the promise of your future. It's not just information...it's transformation.

If something inside you knows there is more — more peace, more joy, more impact — then this book was written for you. The person you're becoming is worth the work. And the transformation God is bringing forth in your life will bless you, and everyone connected to you.

Your journey to your best self begins now.

Get your copy of "Transformation: Change Begins Within — The Journey To Your Best Self." Available on Amazon and wherever books are sold.

https://www.amazon.com/dp/B0DRYR33HK

https://www.dlscreativeworks.com

CONNECT WITH THE AUTHOR

If this book has encouraged or strengthened your prayer life, I would be grateful if you would take a moment to leave a brief review. Your words help others who are searching for deeper intimacy with God discover this message. Thank you for your support.

Grace and peace to you. Thank you for allowing this book to be part of your spiritual journey. It is an honor to walk with you, even in these pages, as you seek deeper intimacy with God.

If you have reflections to share, questions stirred by what you've read, or simply desire to stay connected, I welcome the opportunity to hear from you through the platforms below.

May we continue to grow together in faith, prayer, and the love of Christ.

A SMALL FAVOR

FACEBOOK
https://www.facebook.com/DrLeeSimpson

TWITTER
@drLSimpson
https://twitter.com/drLSimpson

EMAIL

Lifebooks@dlscreativeworks.com

Website Link For Books By Dr. Lee A. Simpson

www.ingramcontent.com/pod-product-compliance
Lightning Source LLC
Chambersburg PA
CBHW061427160726
47995CB00003B/782